Pocket Glossary
of
Health Information
Management
and Technology

American Health Information
Management Association®

ISBN 1-58426-158-7
AHIMA Product No. AB105205

Kenneth Zielske, DIRECTOR OF PUBLICATIONS
Claire Blondeau, PROJECT EDITOR
Melissa Ulbricht, EDITORIAL/PRODUCTION
                    COORDINATOR
Elizabeth Lund, ASSISTANT EDITOR

2 3 4 5 6 7 8 9 10

American Health Information Management Association
233 North Michigan Avenue, Suite 2150
Chicago, Illinois 60601-5800
http://www.ahima.org

INTRODUCTION

I t is said that one of the characteristics of a profession is that it has a unique vocabulary, and health information management is no exception. This *Pocket Glossary for Health Information Management and Technology* is a compilation of the concepts and terms commonly used by professionals in the health information management (HIM) field. The *Pocket Glossary* brings these all together in one convenient reference for use by HIM practitioners, educators, students, researchers, and any health care professional with an interest in HIM practice. Terms and concepts reflect the breadth of practice drawing from the fields of medicine, healthcare management, computer science and their application to health information management and technology.

This versatile desk reference is used to:

1. Define and explain the terms and concepts of the field
2. Provide preferred terms and synonyms to frame research and Internet searches
3. Understand the subject headings that frame HIM practice
4. Explain commonly used acronyms and abbreviations
5. Find key people and organizations in HIM

DEVELOPMENT OF THE *POCKET GLOSSARY*

This reference was developed through comprehensive review of the books and articles of the HIM field and publications from other relevant healthcare domains. Each term was added because of its importance to the field and its value as a subject heading in health information management, including health information technology fields of study.

The *Pocket Guide for Health Information Management and Technology* was reviewed thoroughly by practitioners and educators in the field to ensure that it includes accurate and current technical content, and is comprehensive. Every attempt was made to capture the scope of specialty practice areas in HIM. It was designed to be a useful and useable reference tool for everyone who works—or aspires to work—in this exciting field.

FORMAT OF THE *POCKET GLOSSARY*

For ease of use, the *Pocket Glossary* is organized with many assists:

1. The terms are arranged alphabetically
2. A "See" instruction directs you to related term or terms
3. Acronyms are integrated into the alphabetic Glossary and a "See" reference gets you to the correct spelled-out term with its definition
4. Concepts that are numbers are spelled out and found in alphabetic order

We took great care to capture all or most of the relevant terms, but we may have missed some in these fast-changing times. This publication is not a static resource; it will grow and change and these will be reflected in future editions which we plan to publish on a regular basis.

Please help us make this *the* essential reference for the field by sharing your comments and suggestions. These may be suggestions for additional terms or concepts, or suggested revisions to any of the terms and concepts and their definitions. Please direct these to:

AHIMA Publications Editor

American Health Information Management Association

233 North Michigan Avenue, Suite 2150

Chicago, IL 60601-5800

Or by e-mail to publications@ahima.org

ACKNOWLEDGMENTS

This *Pocket Guide* is the collaborative effort of many. We thank the many authors who directly or indirectly contributed to this *Pocket Glossary*. We thank the reviewers who guided our team throughout its writing. We thank those involved in work groups, volunteers, authors, the AHIMA professional practice staff and AHIMA's outstanding publications team. Together they have made an important contribution to the body of knowledge for the profession.

With sincere thanks,

Linda L. Kloss, MA, RHIA
AHIMA CHIEF EXECUTIVE OFFICER

Glossary

A **AAHC:** *See* **Accreditation Association for Ambulatory Health Care**

AAHP: *See* **American Association of Health Plans**

AAMC: *See* **American Association of Medical Colleges**

AAMRL: *See* **American Association of Medical Record Librarians**

AAMT: *See* **American Association of Medical Transcription**

Abbreviated Injury Scale (AIS): A set of numbers used in a trauma registry to indicate the nature and severity of injuries by body system

ABC: *See* **activity-based costing**

Ability tests: Tests used to assess the skills an individual already possesses; *See* **performance tests**

ABN: *See* **advanced beneficiary notice**

Abnormal Involuntary Movement Scale (AIMS): A standardized form that can be used in facilities to document involuntary movements

Abortion: The expulsion or extraction of all (complete) or any part (incomplete) of the placenta or membranes, without an identifiable fetus or with a liveborn infant or a stillborn infant weighing less than 500 grams

Abstract: Brief summary of the major parts of a research study

Abstracting: 1. The process of extracting information from a document to create a brief summary of a patient's illness, treatment, and outcome   2. The process of extracting elements of data from a source document or database and entering them into an automated system

Abuses: Coding errors that occur without intent to defraud the government

Accept assignment: A term used to refer to a provider's or a supplier's acceptance of the allowed charges (from a fee schedule) as payment in full for services or materials provided

Acceptance theory of authority: A management theory that is based on the principle that employees have the freedom to choose whether they will follow managerial directions

Access: The ability of a subject to view, change, or communicate with an object in a computer system

Access control: 1. A computer software program designed to prevent unauthorized use of an information resource 2. The process of designing, implementing, and monitoring a system for guaranteeing that only individuals who have a legitimate need are allowed to view or amend specific data sets

Access control grid: A tabular representation of the levels of authorization granted to users of a computer system's information and resources

Access control system: A system that defines who has access to what information in a computer system and specifies each user's rights and/or restrictions with respect to that information

Accession number: A number assigned to each case as it is entered in a cancer registry

Accession registry: A list of cases in a cancer registry in the order in which they were entered

Accidents/incidents: Those mishaps, misfortunes, mistakes, events, or occurrences that can happen during the normal daily routines and activities in the long-term care setting

Account: A subdivision of assets, liabilities, and equities in an organization's financial management system

Accountable: Required to answer to a supervisor for performance results

Accountable health plan: *See* **integrated provider organization**

Accounting: 1. The process of collecting, recording, and reporting an organization's financial data 2. A list of all disclosures made of a patient's health information

Accounting entity: The business structure, including the activities and records to be maintained for the preparation of an individual organization's financial statements

Accounting period: The entire process of identifying and recording a transaction, and ultimately reporting it as part of an organization's financial statement

Accounting rate of return: The projected annual cash inflows, minus any applicable depreciation, divided by the initial investment

Accounts Not Selected for Billing Report: A daily financial report used to track the many reasons why accounts may not be ready for billing

Accounts payable (A/P): Records of the payments owed by an organization to other entities

Accounts receivable (A/R): Records of the payments owed to the organization by outside entities such as third-party payers and patients

Accreditation: 1. A voluntary process of institutional or organizational review in which a quasi independent body created for this purpose periodically evaluates the quality of the entity's work against preestablished written criteria   2. A determination by an accrediting body that an eligible organization, network, program, group, or individual complies with applicable standards

Accreditation Association for Ambulatory Health Care (AAAHC): A professional organization that offers accreditation programs for ambulatory and outpatient organizations such as single-specialty and multi-specialty group practices, ambulatory surgery centers, college/university health services, and community health centers

Accreditation organization: A professional organization that establishes the standards against which healthcare organizations are measured and conducts periodical assessments of the performance of individual healthcare organizations

Accreditation standards: Preestablished statements of the criteria against which the performance of participating healthcare organizations will be assessed during a voluntary accreditation process

Accredited Standards Committee (ASC) X12N: A committee of the National Standards Institute that develops and maintains standards for the electronic exchange of business transactions, such as 837—Health Care Claim, 835—Health Care Claim Payment/Advice, and others

Accrediting body: A professional organization that establishes the standards against which healthcare organizations are measured and conducts periodic assessment of the performance of individual healthcare organizations

Accrual accounting: A method of accounting that requires business organizations to report income in the period earned and to deduct expenses in the period incurred

Accuracy: A characteristic of data that are free from significant error and are up-to-date and representative of relevant facts

ACGs: *See* **adjusted clinical groups**

ACHE: *See* **American College of Healthcare Executives**

Acid-test ratio: A ratio in which the sum of cash plus short-term investments plus net current receivables is divided by total current liabilities

Acknowledgement: A form that provides a mechanism for the resident to acknowledge receipt of important information

Acquired immunodeficiency syndrome (AIDS): A retroviral disease caused by infection with human immunodeficiency virus (HIV)

Acquisition: Purchase

ACR-NEMA: *See* **American College of Radiology-National Electrical Manufacturers Association**

ACS: *See* **American College of Surgeons**

Action steps: Specific plans an organization intends to accomplish in the near future as an effort toward achieving its long-term strategic plan

Active listening: The application of effective verbal communications skills as evidenced by the listener's restatement of what the speaker said

Activities of daily living (ADL): The basic activities of self-care, including grooming, bathing, ambulating, toileting, and eating

Activity-based budget: A budget based on activities or projects rather than on functions or departments

Activity-based costing (ABC): An economic model that traces the costs or resources necessary for a product or customer

Activity date or status: The element in the chargemaster that indicates the most recent activity of an item

Actor: The role a user plays in a system

Actual charge: A physician's actual fee for service at the time an insurance claim is submitted to an insurance company, a government payer, or a health maintenance organization; may differ from the allowable charge

Acute care: Medical care of a limited duration that is provided in a an inpatient hospital setting to diagnose and/or treat an injury or a short-term illness

Acute care prospective payment system: The reimbursement system for inpatient hospital services provided to Medicare and Medicaid beneficiaries that is based on the use of diagnosis-related groups as a classification tool

ADA: *See* **American Dental Association**

ADA: *See* **Americans with Disabilities Act**

Adjunct diagnostic or therapeutic unit: An organized unit of an inpatient hospital (other than an operating room, delivery room, or medical care unit) with facilities and personnel to aid physicians in the diagnosis and treatment of illnesses or injuries through the performance of diagnostic or therapeutic procedures; *See* **ancillary unit**

Adjusted clinical groups (ACGs): A classification that groups individuals according to resource requirements and reflects the clinical severity differences among the specific groups; formerly called ambulatory care groups

Adjusted historic payment base (AHPB): The weighted average prevailing charge for a physician service applied in a locality for 1991 and adjusted to reflect payments for services with charges below the prevailing charge levels and other payment limits; determined without regard to physician specialty and reviewed and updated yearly since 1992

Adjusted hospital autopsy rate: The proportion of hospital autopsies performed following the deaths of patients whose bodies are available for autopsy

Adjustment: The process of writing off an unpaid balance on a patient account to make the account balance

ADL: *See* **activities of daily living**

Administrative controls: Policies and procedures that address the management of computer resources

Administrative information: Information used for administrative and healthcare operations purposes such as billing and quality oversight

Administrative information systems: A category of healthcare information systems that supports human resources management, financial management, executive decision support, and other business-related functions

Administrative law: A body of rules and regulations developed by various administrative entities empowered by Congress; falls under the umbrella of public law

Administrative management theory: A subdivision of classical management theory that emphasizes the total organization rather than the individual worker and delineates the major management functions

Administrative services: Business-related services provided by an insurance organization to self-insured employers or other parties according to an administrative services only contract (for example, actuarial support, benefit plan design, claims processing, data recovery and analysis, employee benefits communication, financial advice, medical care conversions, stop-loss coverage, and other services as requested)

Administrative services only (ASO) contract: An agreement between an employer and an insurance organization to administer the employer's self-insured health plan

Admission agreement: A legal contract signed by the resident that specifies the long-term care facility's responsibilities and fees for providing healthcare and other services

Admission date: In the home health prospective payment system, the date of first service; in the acute care prospective payment system, the year, month, and day of inpatient admission, beginning with a hospital's formal acceptance of a patient who is to receive healthcare services while receiving room, board, and continuous nursing services

Admissions and readmissions processing policy: A policy that provides the guidelines that are required when a resident is admitted or readmitted to the facility

Admission type: The classification of inpatient admissions used for completing CMS-1450 forms

Admission utilization review: A review of planned services (intensity of service) and/or a patient's condition (severity of illness) to determine whether care must be delivered in an acute care setting

Admitting diagnosis: A provisional description of the reason why a patient requires care in an inpatient hospital setting

ADS: *See* **alternative delivery system**

Adult day care: Group or individual therapeutic services provided during the daytime hours to persons outside their homes; usually provided for individuals with geriatric or psychiatric illnesses

Adult health questionnaire: *See* **patient history questionnaire**

Advance beneficiary notice (ABN): A statement signed by the patient when he or she is notified by the provider, prior to a service or procedure being done, that Medicare may not reimburse the provider for the service, wherein the patient indicates that he will be responsible for any charges

Advanced decision support: Automated clinical practice guidelines that are built in to electronic health record systems and designed to support clinical decision making

Advance directive: A legal, written document that describes the patient's preferences regarding future healthcare or stipulates the person who is authorized to make medical decisions in the event the patient is incapable of communicating his or her preferences

Advanced practice registered nurse (ARPN): The term being increasingly used by legislative and governing bodies to describe the collection of registered nurses that practice in the extended role beyond the normal role of basic registered nursing

Adverse selection: A situation in which individuals who are sicker than the general population are attracted to a health insurance plan, with adverse effects on the plan's costs

Affinity grouping: A technique for organizing similar ideas together in natural groupings

Aftercare: Healthcare services that are provided to a patient after a period of hospitalization or rehabilitation and are administered with the objective of improving or restoring health to the degree that aftercare is no longer needed

Against medical advice (AMA): The discharge status of patients who leave a hospital after signing a form that releases the hospital from any responsibility or who leave a hospital without notifying hospital personnel

Age Discrimination in Employment Act: Federal legislation that prohibits employment discrimination against persons between the ages of forty and seventy and restricts mandatory retirement requirements except where age is a bona fide occupational qualification

Agency for Healthcare Research and Quality (AHRQ): The branch of the United States Public Health Service that supports general health research and distributes research findings and treatment guidelines with the goal of improving the quality, appropriateness, and effectiveness of healthcare services

Agenda for Change: An initiative undertaken by the Joint Commission on Accreditation of Healthcare Organizations that focused on changing the emphasis of the accreditation process from structure to outcomes

Aggregate data: Data extracted from individual health records and combined to form deidentified information about groups of patients that can be compared and analyzed

Aging of accounts: The practice of counting the days, generally in thirty-day increments, from the time a bill was sent to the payer to the current day

AHA: *See* **American Hospital Association**

AHIMA: *See* **American Health Information Management Association**

AHPB: *See* **adjusted historic payment base**

AHRQ: *See* **Agency for Healthcare Research and Quality**

AI: *See* **artificial intelligence**

AIDS: *See* **acquired immunodeficiency syndrome**

AIMS: *See* **Abnormal Involuntary Movement Scale**

Alarm: A type of warning that is generated by an automated medical device

Alert: A software-generated warning that is based on a set of clinical rules built in to a healthcare information system

Algorithm: A procedure for solving a mathematical problem in a finite number of steps that frequently involves repetition of an operation

Algorithmic translation: A process that involves the use of algorithms to translate or map clinical nomenclatures among each other or to map natural language to a clinical nomenclature or vice versa

Alias: A name added to, or substituted for, the proper name of a person; an assumed name

Alias policy: A policy that is implemented when resident confidentiality is require by the resident, family, or responsible party

Allied health professional: A credentialed healthcare worker who is not a physician, nurse, psychologist, or pharmacist (for example, a physical therapist, dietitian, social worker, or occupational therapist)

Allowable charge: Average or maximum amount a third party payer will reimburse providers for a service; *See* **allowable fee**

Allowable fee: *See* **allowable charge**

All-patient diagnosis-related groups (AP-DRGs): A case-mix system developed by 3M and used in a number of state reimbursement systems to classify non-Medicare discharges for reimbursement purposes

All-patient refined diagnosis-related groups (APR-DRGs): An expansion of the inpatient classification system that includes four distinct subclasses (minor, moderate, major, and extreme) based on the severity of the patient's illness

ALOS: *See* **average length of stay**

Alphabetic filing system: A system of health record identification and storage that uses the patient's last name as the first component of identification and his or her first name and middle name or initial for further definition

Alphanumeric filing system: A system of health record identification and storage that uses a combination of alphabetic letters (usually the first two letters of the patient's last name) and numbers to identify individual records

Alternative delivery system (ADS): A type of healthcare delivery systems in which health services are provided in settings such as skilled and intermediary facilities, hospice programs, nonacute outpatient programs, and home health programs, which are more cost-effective than in the inpatient setting

Alternative hypothesis: A hypothesis that states that there is an association between independent and dependent variables

AMA: *See* **against medical advice**

AMA: *See* **American Medical Association**

Ambulatory care: Preventive or corrective healthcare services provided on a nonresident basis in a provider's office, clinic setting, or hospital outpatient setting

Ambulatory care organization: A healthcare provider or facility that offers preventive, diagnostic, therapeutic, and rehabilitative services to individuals not classified as inpatients or residents

Ambulatory patient group (APG): A classification system used until 2000 to categorize ambulatory patients according to case types as a pricing mechanism for outpatient services provided to Medicare and Medicaid beneficiaries

Ambulatory payment classification (APC) relative weight: A number reflecting the expected resource consumption of cases associated with each APC, relative to the average of all APCs, that is used in determining payment for hospital outpatient services provided to Medicare and Medicaid beneficiaries

Ambulatory payment classification (APC) system: The prospective payment system used since 2000 for reimbursement of hospitals for outpatient services provided to Medicare and Medicaid beneficiaries

Ambulatory surgery: An elective surgical procedure performed on a patient who is classified as an outpatient and who is usually released from the surgical facility on the day of surgery

Ambulatory surgical center (ASC): Under Medicare, an outpatient surgical facility that has its own national identifier; is a separate entity with respect to its licensure, accreditation, governance, professional supervision, administrative functions, clinical services, record keeping, and financial and accounting systems; has as its sole purpose the provision of services in connection with surgical procedures that do not require inpatient hospitalization; and meets the conditions and requirements set forth in the Medicare Conditions of Participation

Ambulatory surgical center (ASC) list: The list of surgical procedures that the Centers for Medicare and Medicaid Services considers safe and appropriate in an outpatient setting and for which Medicare pays a prospectively determined ASC facility fee

Ambulatory surgical center (ASC) services: Services that a Medicare-approved ambulatory surgical center provides in connection with procedures on the ASC list

American Association for Medical Transcription (AAMT): The national professional association for medical transcriptionists

American Association of Health Plans (AAHP): The trade organization for health maintenance organizations, preferred provider organizations, and other network-based health plans created by the merger of the Group Health Association of America and the American Managed Care and Review Association

American Association of Medical Colleges (AAMC): The organization established in 1876 to standardize the curriculum for medical schools in the United States and to promote the licensure of physicians

American Association of Medical Record Librarians (AAMRL): The name adopted by the Association of

Record Librarians of North America in 1944; precursor of the **American Health Information Management Association**

American College of Healthcare Executives (ACHE): The national professional organization of healthcare administrators that provides certification services for its members and promotes excellence in the field

American College of Radiology — National Electrical Manufacturers Association (ACR–NEMA): The professional organizations (ACR) and trade associations (NEMA) that work collaboratively to develop digital imaging standards

American College of Surgeons (ACS): The scientific and educational association of surgeons formed to improve the quality of surgical care by setting high standards for surgical education and practice

American College of Surgeons Commission on Cancer: The organization that approves cancer-related programs, including cancer registries and trauma centers

American Dental Association (ADA): A professional dental association dedicated to the public's oral health, ethics, science, and professional advancement

American Health Information Management Association (AHIMA): The professional membership organization for managers of health record services and healthcare information systems as well as coding services; provides accreditation, certification, and educational services

American Hospital Association (AHA): The national trade organization that provides education, conducts research, and represents the hospital industry's interests in national legislative matters; membership includes individual healthcare organizations as well as individual healthcare professionals working in specialized areas of hospitals, such as risk management

American Medical Association (AMA): The national professional membership organization for physicians that distributes scientific information to its members and the public, informs members of legislation related to health and medicine, and represents the medical profession's interests in national legislative matters

American Medical Informatics Association (AMIA): The membership organization composed of individuals, institutions, and corporations that develop and use information technologies in healthcare

American Medical Record Association (AMRA): The name adopted by the American Association of Medical Record Librarians in 1970; precursor of the **American Health Information Management Association**

American National Standards Institute (ANSI): The organization that accredits all U.S. standards development organizations to ensure that they are following due process in promulgating standards

American Nurses Association (ANA): The national professional membership association of nurses that works for the improvement of health standards and the availability of healthcare services, fosters high professional standards for the nursing profession, and advances the economic and general welfare of nurses

American Occupational Therapy Association (AOTA): The nationally recognized professional association of more than 40,000 occupational therapists, occupational therapy assistants, and students of occupational therapy

American Osteopathic Association (AOA): The professional association of osteopathic physicians, surgeons, and graduates of approved colleges of osteopathic medicine that inspects and accredits osteopathic colleges and hospitals

American Physical Therapy Association (APTA): The national professional organization whose goal is to foster advancements in physical therapy practice, research, and education

American Psychiatric Association (APA): The international professional association of psychiatrists and related medical specialists that works to ensure humane care and effective treatment for all persons with mental disorders, including mental retardation and substance-related disorders

American Psychological Association (APA): The professional organization that aims to advance psychology as a science and profession and promotes health, education, and human welfare

American Society for Healthcare Risk Management (ASHRM): The professional society for healthcare risk management professionals that is affiliated with the American Hospital Association and provides educational tools and networking opportunities for its members

American Society for Quality (ASQ): A quality improvement organization whose members' interests are related to statistical process control, quality cost measurement and control, total quality management, failure analysis, and zero defects

American Society for Testing and Materials (ASTM): A national organization whose purpose is to establish standards on materials, products, systems, and services

American Society for Testing and Materials Committee E31 (ASTM E31)—Healthcare Informatics: A committee within the American Society for Testing and Materials that creates standards on the content, structure, and functionality of electronic health record systems, health information confidentiality policies and procedures, health data security, and the exchange of information across clinical systems, such as laboratory devices with information systems

American Society for Testing and Materials Standard E1384 (ASTM E1384)—Standard Guide for Description of Content and Structure of an Automated Primary Record of Care: A standard that identifies the basic information to be included in electronic health records and requires the information to be organized into categories

American Standard Code for Information Interchange (ASCII): A technique whereby computers transform a binary code they can understand into characters that humans can understand

Americans with Disabilities Act (ADA): Federal legislation that makes it illegal to discriminate against individuals with disabilities in employment, public accommodations, public services, transportation, and telecommunications

AMIA: *See* **American Medical Information Association**

AMLOS: *See* **arithmetic mean length of stay**

AMRA: *See* **American Medical Record Association**

ANA: *See* **American Nurses Association**

Analog: Data or information that is *not* represented in an encoded, computer-readable format

Analysis of discharged health records policy: A policy that outlines steps to be taken to process discharged resident records

Analysis phase: The first phase of the systems development life cycle during which the scope of the project is defined, project goals are identified, current systems are evaluated, and user needs are identified

Analysis session: The process of mining a data segment

Ancillary packaging: The inclusion of routinely performed support services in the reimbursement classification of a healthcare procedure or service

Ancillary service visit: The appearance of an outpatient in a unit of a hospital or outpatient facility to receive services, tests, or procedures; ordinarily not counted as an encounter for healthcare services

Ancillary services: Tests and procedures ordered by a physician to provide information for use in patient diagnosis or treatment

Ancillary unit: *See* **adjunct diagnostic or therapeutic unit**

Androgynous leadership: Leadership in which cultural stereotyped masculine and feminine styles are integrated into a more effective hybrid style

Anesthesia death rate: The ratio of deaths caused by anesthetic agents to the number of anesthesias administered during a specified period of time

Anesthetic risk: The risk of harm resulting from the administration of anesthetic agents

ANN: *See* **artificial neural network**

ANSI: *See* **American National Standards Institute**

Antipsychotic Dyskinesia Identification System: One of several standardized forms for assessing and documenting abnormal movements (of face, eyes, mouth/tongue, or body) that may occur in the course of treatment with some psychotropic medications; *See* **discus monitoring form**

Antipsychotic medications: Drugs that are used in the management of psychotic conditions, bipolar disorders, or major depression with psychotic features

AOA: *See* **American Osteopathic Association**

AOTA: *See* **American Occupational Therapy Association**

A/P: *See* **accounts payable**

APA: *See* **American Psychiatric Association**

APA: *See* **American Psychological Association**

APC relative weight: *See* **ambulatory payment classification relative weight**

APC system: *See* **ambulatory payment classification system**

AP-DRGs: *See* **all-patient diagnosis-related groups**

APG: *See* **ambulatory payment group**

API: *See* **Application Programming Interface**

Appeal: A request for reconsideration of a negative claim decision

Appellate court: In a state court system, the court that hears appeals of final judgments from state trial courts

Application controls: Security strategies, such as password management, included in application software and computer programs

Application Programming Interface (API): A set of definitions of the ways in which one piece of computer software communicates with another, or a programmer makes requests of the operating system or another application; operates outside the realm of the direct user interface

Applications and data criticality analysis: A covered entity's formal assessment of the sensitivity, vulnerabilities, and security of its programs and the information it generates, receives, manipulates, stores, and/or transmits

Application service provider (ASP): A third-party service company that delivers, manages, and remotely hosts standardized applications software via a network through an outsourcing contract based on fixed, monthly usage or transaction-based pricing

Applied artificial intelligence: An area of computer science that deals with algorithms and computer systems that exhibit the characteristics commonly associated with human intelligence

Applied Healthcare Informatics: Automated information systems applied to healthcare delivery business and workflow processes, including the diagnosis, therapy, and systems of managing health data and information within the healthcare setting

Applied research: A type of research that focuses on the use of scientific theories to improve actual practice as in medical research applied to the treatment of patients

Appreciative inquiry: An organizational development technique in which successful practices are identified and expanded throughout the organization

APR: *See* **average payment rate**

APR-DRGs: *See* **all-patient refined diagnosis-related groups**

APS: *See* **Attending Physician Statement**

APTA: *See* **American Physical Therapy Association**

Aptitude tests: Tests that assess an individual's general ability to learn a new skill

A/R: *See* **accounts receivable**

AR: *See* **attributable risk**

Arbitration: A proceeding in which disputes are submitted to a third party or a panel of experts outside the judicial trial system

Architecture: The configuration, structure, and relationships of hardware (the machinery of the computer including input/output devices, storage devices, and so on) in an information system

ARD: *See* **assessment reference date**

Arden syntax: A standard for medical knowledge representation for use in clinical decision support systems

Arithmetic mean length of stay (AMLOS): The average length of stay for all patients

ARPN: *See* **advanced practice registered nurse**

Artificial intelligence (AI): High-level information technologies used in developing machines that imitate human qualities such as learning and reasoning

Artificial neural network (ANN): A computational technique based on artificial intelligence and machine learning in which the structure and operation are inspired by the properties and operation of the human brain

ASC: *See* **Accredited Standards Committee**

ASC: *See* **ambulatory surgical center**

ASCII: *See* **American Standard Code for Information Interchange**

ASC list: *See* **ambulatory surgical center list**

ASC services: *See* **ambulatory surgical center services**

ASHRM: *See* **American Society for Healthcare Risk Management**

ASO contract: *See* **administrative services only contract**

ASP: *See* **application service provider**

ASQ: *See* **American Society for Quality**

Assembler: A computer program that translates assembly-language instructions into machine language

Assembly language: A second-generation computer programming language that uses simple phrases rather than the complex series of switches used in machine language

Assessment: The systematic collection and review of information pertaining to an individual who wants to receive healthcare services or enter a healthcare setting

Assessment completion date: According to the Centers for Medicare and Medicaid Services' instructions, the date by which a Minimum Data Set for Long-Term Care must be completed; that is, within fourteen days of admission to a long-term care facility

Assessment final completion date: The date (within thirty-two days of the assessment's final completion date) on which the Centers for Medicare and Medicaid requires Minimum Data Set for Long-Term Care assessments to be electronically submitted to the facility's state Minimum Data Set for Long-Term Care database

Assessment indicator code: A component of the code used for Medicare billing by long-term care facilities

Assessment locking: A term that refers to the Centers for Medicare and Medicaid Services' requirement that long-term care facilities must encode Minimum Data Set assessments in a computerized file and edit the data items for compliance with data specifications

Assessment reference date (ARD): The date (MDS data item A3a) that sets the designated end point of resident observation for all staff participating in the assessment

Assets: The human, financial, and physical resources of an organization

Assignment of benefits: The transfer of one's interest or policy benefits to another party, typically the payment of medical benefits directly to a provider of care

Assisted living: A type of freestanding long-term care facility where residents receive necessary medical services but retain a degree of independence

Association rule analysis: The process of extracting useful if/then rules from data based on statistical significance; *See* **rule induction**

Assumption coding: The practice of assigning codes on the basis of clinical signs, symptoms, test findings, or treatments without supporting physician documentation

Assumptions: Undetermined aspects of a project that are considered to be true (for example, assuming that project team members have the right skill set to perform their duties)

ASTM: *See* **American Society for Testing and Materials**

ASTM E1384: *See* **American Society for Testing and Materials Standard E1384 Standard Guide for Description of Content and Structure of an Automated Primary Record of Care**

ASTM E31: *See* **American Society for Testing and Materials Committee E31-Healthcare Informatics**

Asynchronous: Occurring at different times

Asynchronous transfer mode (ATM): A topology for transmitting data across large wide-area networks

Atlas System: A severity-of-illness system commonly used in the United States and Canada

ATM: *See* **asynchronous transfer mode**

At risk contract: A type of managed care contract between Medicare and a payer or a payer and a provider according to which patients receive care during the entire term of the contract even if actual costs exceed the payment established by the agreement

Attending physician: The physician primarily responsible for the care and treatment of a patient

Attending physician identification: The unique national identification number assigned to the clinician of record at discharge who is responsible for the inpatient discharge summary

Attending Physician Statement (APS): The standardized insurance claim form created in 1958 by the Health Insurance Association of America and the American Medical Association; *See* **COMB-1 form**

Attributable risk (AR): A measure of the impact of a disease on a population (for example, measuring additional risk of illness as a result of exposure to a risk factor)

Attributes: 1. Data elements within an entity that become the column or field names when the entity relationship diagram is implemented as a relational database   2. Properties or characteristics of concepts; in SNOMED CT, attributes are used to characterize and define concepts

Attrition: *See* **mortality**

Audit: A review process conducted by healthcare facilities (internally and/or externally) to identify variations from established baselines; *See* **external review**

Audit control: A method for monitoring attempts to gain access to a computer information system

Audit trail: A chronological set of computerized records that provides evidence of information system activity (logins and log-outs, file accesses) that is used to determine security violations

Authenticated: Confirmed by signing

Authentication: 1. The process of identifying the source of health record entries by attaching a handwritten signature, the author's initials, or an electronic signature 2. Proof of authorship that ensures, as much as possible, that log-ins and messages from a user originate from an authorized source

Author: The originator of a health record entry

Authority: The right to make decisions and take actions necessary to carry out assigned tasks

Authorization: The granting of permission to disclose confidential information; as defined in terms of the HIPAA privacy rule, an individual's formal, written permission to use or disclose his or her personally identifiable health information for purposes other than treatment, payment, or healthcare operations

Authorization management: The process of protecting the security and privacy of the confidential data in a database

Autoauthentication: A procedure that allows dictated reports to be considered automatically signed unless the health information management department is notified of needed revisions within a certain time limit

Autocoding: The process of extracting and translating dictated and then transcribed free-text data (or dictated and then computer-generated discrete data) into ICD-9-CM and CPT evaluation and management codes for billing and coding purposes

Autodialing system: A method used to automatically call and remind patients of upcoming appointments

Automated forms processing technology: Technology that allows users to electronically enter data into online, digital forms and electronically extract data from online, digital forms for data collection or manipulation; *See* **e-forms technology**

Automatic log-off: A security procedure that ends a computer session after a predetermined period of inactivity

Autonomy: A core ethical principle centered on the individual's right to self-determination that includes respect for the individual; in clinical applications, the patient's right to determine what does or does not happen to him or her in terms of healthcare

Autopsy rate: The proportion or percentage of deaths in a healthcare organization that are followed by the performance of autopsy

Autopsy report: Written documentation of the findings from a postmortem pathological examination

Available for hospital autopsy: A situation in which the required conditions have been met to allow an autopsy to be performed on a hospital patient who has died

Average daily census: The mean number of hospital inpatients present in the hospital each day for a given period of time

Average duration of hospitalization: *See* **average length of stay**

Average length of stay (ALOS): The mean length of stay for hospital inpatients discharged during a given period of time

Average payment rate (APR): The amount of money the Centers for Medicare and Medicaid could pay a health maintenance organization for services rendered to Medicare recipients under a risk contract

Average record delinquency rate: The monthly average number of discharges divided by the monthly average number of delinquent records

Average wholesale price (AWP): The price commonly used when negotiating pharmacy contracts

Awareness training: Training designed to help individuals understand and respond to information technology concerns

AWP: *See* **average wholesale price**

Backbone: A high-speed medium used as the main trunk in a computer network to transmit high volumes of traffic

Backup: The process of maintaining a copy of all software and data for use in the case that the primary source becomes compromised

Backward compatibility: The capability of a software or hardware product to work with earlier versions of itself

Bad debt: The receivables of an organization that are uncollectible

Balance billing: A reimbursement method that allows providers to bill patients for charges in excess of the amount paid by the patients' health plan or other third-party payer (not allowed under Medicare or Medicaid)

Balanced Budget Act (BBA) of 1997: Public Law 105-33 enacted by Congress on August 5, 1997, that mandated a number of additions, deletions, and revisions to the original Medicare and Medicaid legislation; the legislation that added penalties for healthcare fraud and abuse to the Medicare and Medicaid programs

Balanced Budget Refinement Act (BBRA) of 1999: The amended version of the Balanced Budget Act of 1997 that authorizes implementation of a per-discharge prospective payment system for care provided to Medicare beneficiaries by inpatient rehabilitation facilities

Balanced score card (BSC): A strategic planning tool that identifies performance measures related to strategic goals

Balance sheet: A report that shows the total dollar amounts in accounts, expressed in accounting equation format, at a specific point in time

Baldridge Award: A congressional award that recognizes excellence in several areas of business

Bandwidth: The range of frequencies a device or communication medium is capable of carrying

Bar chart: A graphic technique used to display frequency distributions of nominal or ordinal data that fall into categories; *See* **bar graph**

Bar coding technology: A method of encoding data that consists of parallel arrangements of dark elements, referred to as bars, and light elements, referred to as spaces, and interpreting the data for automatic identification and data collection purposes

Bar graph: *See* **bar chart**

Baseline: The original estimates for a project's schedule, work, and cost

Baseline adjustment for volume and intensity of service: An adjustment to the conversion factor needed to fulfill the statutory budget neutrality requirement

Basic research: A type of research that focuses on the development and refinement of theories

Batch processing: The grouping of computer tasks to be run at one time; common in mainframe systems where the user did not interact with the computer in real time but, instead, data were often processed at night and produced time-delayed output

BBA of 1997: *See* **Balanced Budget Act of 1997**

BBRA of 1999: *See* **Balanced Budget Refinement Act of 1999**

BC/BS: *See* **Blue Cross and Blue Shield**

BC/BS Service Benefit Plan: *See* **Blue Cross and Blue Shield Federal Employee Program (FEP)**

Bed capacity: The number of beds that a facility has been designed and constructed to house

Bed complement: *See* **bed count**

Bed count: The number of inpatient beds set up and staffed for use on a given day; *See* **bed complement**

Bed count day: A unit of measure that denotes the presence of one inpatient bed (either occupied or vacant) set up and staffed for use in one twenty-four-hour period

Bed occupancy ratio: The proportion of beds occupied, defined as the ratio of inpatient service days to bed count days during a specified period of time

Bed size: The total number of inpatient beds for which a facility is equipped and staffed to provide patient care services

Bed turnover rate: The average number of times a bed changes occupants during a given period of time

Behavioral description interview: An interview format that requires applicants to give specific examples of how they have performed a specific procedure or handled a specific problem in the past

Behavioral health: A broad array of psychiatric services provided in acute, long-term, and ambulatory care settings; includes treatment of mental disorders, chemical dependency, mental retardation, and developmental disabilities as well as cognitive rehabilitation services

Behavioral healthcare organization: An organization that can provide a wide array of services, including diagnosis and treatment for mental disorders, chemical dependency, mental retardation, developmental disabilities, and cognitive rehabilitative services in either an acute, long-term, or ambulatory care setting

Benchmarking: An analysis process that is based on comparison

Benchmarking survey: A survey in which a healthcare facility compares elements of its operation with those of similar healthcare facilities

Beneficence: A legal term that means promoting good for others or providing services that benefit others, such as releasing health information that will help a patient receive care or will ensure payment for services received

Benefit: Healthcare service for which the healthcare insurance company will pay; *See* **covered expenses**

Benefit cap: Total dollar amount that a healthcare insurance company will pay for covered healthcare services during a specified period, such as a year or lifetime

Benefit level: The degree to which a person is entitled to receive services based on his or her contract with a health plan or an insurer

Best practice: Term used to refer to services that have been deemed effective and efficient with certain groups of clients

Bill drop: The point at which a bill is completed and electronically or manually sent to the payer

Bill hold period: The span of time during which a bill is suspended in the billing system awaiting late charges, diagnosis and/or procedure codes, insurance verification, or other required information

Billing audit: *See* **quantitative audit**

Bills of Mortality: Documents used in London during the seventeenth century to identify the most common causes of death

Bioethics: A field of study that applies ethical principles to decisions that affect the lives of humans, such as whether to approve or deny access to health information

Biomedical research: The process of systematically investigating subjects related to the functioning of the human body

Biometric identification system: An identification system that analyzes biological data about users, such as voiceprints, fingerprints, handprint, retinal scan, faceprints, and full-body scans

Biometrics: The physical characteristics of users (such as fingerprints, voiceprints, retinal scans, iris traits) that systems store and use to authenticate identity before allowing the user access to a system

Birth weight: The weight of a neonate (expressed to the nearest gram) determined immediately after delivery or as soon thereafter as feasible

Birth weight of newborn (inpatient): The specific birth weight of the newborn, recorded in grams

Bit: The level of voltage (low or high) in a computer that provides the binary states of 0 and 1 that computers use to represent characters

Bit-mapped data: Data made up of pixels displayed on a horizontal and vertical grid or matrix

Bivariate: An adjective meaning the involvement of two variables

Blanket authorization: An authorization for the release of confidential information from a certain point in time and any time thereafter

Blended learning: A training strategy that uses a combination of techniques—such as lecture, Web-based training, or programmed text—to appeal to a variety of learning styles and maximize the advantages of each training method

Blended rate: A rate assigned to hospitals by the CMS based on cost of living, location, and services provided

Blue Cross and Blue Shield (BC/BS): The first prepaid healthcare plans in the United States; Blue Shield plans traditionally cover hospital care and Blue Cross plans cover physicians' services

Blue Cross and Blue Shield Association: The national association of state and local Blue Cross and Blue Shield plans

Blue Cross and Blue Shield Federal Employee Program (FEP): A federal program that offers a fee-for-service plan with preferred provider organizations and a point-of-service product; *See* **BC/BS Service Benefit Plan**

Board certified: A designation given to a physician or other health professional who has passed an exam from a medical specialty board and is thereby certified to provide care within that specialty

Boarder: An individual such as a parent, caregiver, or other family member who receives lodging at a healthcare facility but is not a patient

Boarder baby: A newborn who remains in the nursery following discharge because the mother is still hospitalized or a premature infant who no longer needs intensive care but remains for observation

Board of directors: The elected or appointed group of officials who bear ultimate responsibility for the successful operation of a healthcare organization; *See* **board of governors** and **board of trustees**

Board of governors: *See* **board of directors**

Board of trustees: *See* **board of directors**

Boot-record infectors: *See* **system infectors**

Bounded rationality: The recognition that decision making is often based on limited time and information about a problem and that many situations are complex and rapidly changing

BPR: *See* **business process reengineering**

Brainstorming: A group problem-solving technique that involves the spontaneous contribution of ideas from all members of the group

Branding communications: Messages sent to increase awareness of, and to enhance the image of, a product in the marketplace

Breach of confidentiality: A violation of a formal or implied contract in which private information belonging to one party, but entrusted to another party, is disclosed by that individual without the consent of the party to whom the information pertains; an unauthorized disclosure of confidential information

Breach of security: A violation of security (for example, when standards of confidentiality are broken)

Break-even analysis: A financial analysis technique for determining the level of sales at which total revenues equal total costs beyond which revenues become profits

Broadband: A type of communications medium that can transmit multiple channels of data simultaneously

Browser: A program that provides a way to view and read documents available on the World Wide Web

BSC: *See* **balanced score card**

Bubble chart: A type of scatter plot with circular symbols used to compare three variables; the area of the circle indicates the value of a third variable

Budget calendar: *See* **budget cycle**

Budget cycle: The process often followed from conceptualizing budget needs through working within the confines of an approved budget; *See* **budget calendar**

Budget neutral: Financial protections to ensure that overall reimbursement under the Ambulatory Payment Classification (APC) system is not greater than it would have been had the system not been in effect

Budget period: A predetermined period of time, such as a fiscal year, in which a project budget will be spent

Bugs: Problems in software that prevent the smooth application of a function

Bundled: The grouping of *Common Procedural Terminology* codes related to a procedure when submitting a claim

Bundled payments: *See* **episode-of-care reimbursement**

Bureaucracy: A formal organizational structure based on a rigid hierarchy of decision making and inflexible rules and procedures

Bus: A type of hardware that controls the flow of commands between the central processor and other components

Business associate: According to the HIPAA privacy rule, an individual (or group) who is not a member of a covered entity's workforce but who helps the covered entity in the performance of various functions involving the use or disclosure of patient-identifiable health information

Business case: An economic argument, or justification, usually for a capital expenditure

Business continuity plan: A program that incorporates policies and procedures for continuing business operations during a computer system shutdown

Business intelligence: The end product or goal of knowledge management

Business process: A set of related policies and procedures that are performed step by step to accomplish a business-related function

Business process management technology: *See* **workflow technology**

Business process reengineering (BPR): The analysis and design of the work flow within and between organizations

Business resumption: The procedure for returning a computer system to its full functionality after unscheduled downtime; similar to disaster recovery

Bylaws: Operating documents that describe the rules and regulations under which a healthcare organization operates; *See* **rules and regulations**

Byte: Eight bits treated as a single unit by a computer to represent a character

C: A high-level programming language that enables programmers to write software instructions that can be translated into machine language to run on different types of computers

CA: *See* **certificate authority**

Cafeteria plan: A health plan that allows employees to choose among two or more benefits

Calculation of inpatient service days: The measurement of the services received by all inpatients in one 24-hour period

Calculation of transfers: A medical care unit that shows transfers on and off the unit as subdivisions of patients admitted to and discharged from the unit

Call center: A central access point to healthcare services in which clinical decision-making algorithms generate a series of questions designed to help a nurse assess a caller's healthcare condition and direct the caller to the appropriate level of service

CAM: *See* **component alignment model**

Cap: A contract maximum

CAP: *See* **College of American Pathologists**

CAP: *See* **corrective action plan**

Capital assets: Physical asset with an estimated useful life of more than 1 year; *See* **fixed assets** and **property, plant, and equipment (PPE)**

Capital budget: The allocation of resources for long-term investments and projects

Capital budget process: A four-stage process organizations follow to determine what capital projects to include in the budget

Capitated patient: A patient enrolled in a managed care program that pays a fixed monthly payment to the patient's identified primary care provider

Capitated payment: A managed care term that refers to the fixed amount a physician or other healthcare provided is paid to provide services to a patient or a group of patients over a prespecified period of time

Capitation: A method of healthcare reimbursement in which an insurance carrier prepays a physician, hospital, or other healthcare provider a fixed amount for a given population without regard to the actual number or nature of healthcare services provided to the population

Care: The management of, responsibility for, or attention to the safety and well-being of other persons in the context of healthcare settings

Care Map: A proprietary care-planning tool similar to a clinical protocol that outlines the major aspects of treatment on the basis of diagnosis or other characteristics of the patient

Care path: A care-planning tool similar to a clinical practice guideline that has a multidisciplinary focus emphasizing the coordination of clinical services; *See* **clinical pathway, critical path,** and **clinical algorithm**

Care plan: The specific goals in the treatment of an individual patient, amended as the patient's condition requires, and the assessment of the outcomes of care; serves as the primary source for ongoing documentation of the resident's care, condition, and needs

Care planning: The process of organizing and documenting the specific goals in the treatment of an individual patient, amending the goals as the patient's condition requires, and assessing the outcomes of care

Care unit: An organizational entity of a healthcare facility; healthcare facilities are organized both physically and functionally into units to provide care

Career development: The process of growing or progressing within one's profession or occupation

Caregiver: 1. Any clinical professional (physician, nurse, technologist, or therapist, for example) who provides care directly to patients   2. A nonprofessional who provides supportive assistance in a residential setting to a relative, friend, or client who is seriously ill

CARF: *See* **Commission on Accreditation of Rehabilitation Facilities**

Carrier, Medicare: An organization under contract with the Centers for Medicare and Medicaid Services to serve as the financial agent that works with providers and the federal government to locally administer Medicare eligibility and payments

Carve-outs: Applicable services that are cut out of the contract and paid at a different rate

Case: Patient, resident, or client with a given condition or disease

Case-based payment: Type of prospective payment method in which the third party payer reimburses the provider a fixed, pre-established payment for each case

Case-control study: A study that investigates the development of disease by amassing volumes of data about factors in the lives of persons with the disease (cases) and persons without the disease; *See* **retrospective study**

Case definition: A method of determining criteria for cases that should be included in a registry

Case fatality rate: The total number of deaths due to a specific illness during a given time period divided by the total number of cases during the same period

Case finding: A method of identifying patients who have been seen and/or treated in a healthcare facility for the particular disease or condition of interest to the registry

Case law: *See* **common law**

Case management: 1. The ongoing, concurrent review performed by clinical professionals to ensure the necessity and effectiveness of the clinical services being provided to a patient   2. A process that integrates and coordinates patient care over time and across multiple sites and providers, especially in complex and high-cost cases   3. The process of developing a specific care plan for a patient that serves as a communication tool to improve quality of care and reduce cost

Case manager: 1. A professional nurse who coordinates the daily progress of a patient population by assessing needs, developing goals, individualizing plans of care on an ongoing basis, and evaluating overall progress 2. A medical professional (usually a nurse or a social worker) who reviews cases to determine the necessity of care and to advise providers on payer's utilization restrictions

Case mix: A description of a patient population based on any number of specific characteristics, including age, gender, type of insurance, diagnosis, risk factors, treatment received, and resources used

Case-mix group payment rate: The predetermined, per-discharge reimbursement amount for each case-mix group that includes all of the inpatient operating and capital costs incurred in furnishing covered rehabilitation services, but not the costs associated with bad debts, approved educational activities, and other costs not paid for under the prospective payment system

Case-mix group relative weights: Factors that account for the variance in cost per discharge and resource utilization among case-mix groups

Case-mix groups (CMGs): The ninety-seven function-related groups into which inpatient rehabilitation facility discharges are classified on the basis of the patient's level of impairment, age, comorbidities, and functional ability and other factors

Case-mix index (CMI): The average relative weight of all cases treated at a given facility or by a given physician, which reflects the resource intensity or clinical severity of a specific group in relation to the other groups in the classification system; calculated by dividing the sum of the weights of diagnosis-related groups for patients discharged during a given period divided by the total number of patients discharged

Case-mix system: A system for grouping cases that are clinically similar and ordinarily consume similar resources;

used to provide information about the types of patients treated by a facility

Case study: A type of nonparticipant observation in which researchers investigate one person, one group, or one institution in depth

Cash: The actual money that has been received and is readily available to pay debts

Cash accounting: A method of accounting that is used most frequently in a sole proprietorship or a small business environment that recognizes income and expense transactions when cash is received or cash is paid out

Cash budget: A forecast of needs for available funds throughout the year

Cash conversion cycle: The period that refers to expenditures needed to provide services to patients through the reimbursement or collection of fees for those provided services

Cash flow: The availability of money to pay the organization's bills (receipts minus disbursements)

Catastrophic coverage: *See* **major medical insurance**

Catastrophic expense limit: Specific amount, in a certain time frame such as one year, beyond which all covered healthcare services for that policyholder or dependent are paid at 100 percent by the healthcare insurance plan; *See* **maximum out-of-pocket cost** and **stop-loss benefit**

Categorical data: Four types of data (nominal, ordinal, interval, and ratio) that represent values or observations that can be sorted into a category; *See* **scales of measurement**

Categorically needy eligibility: Categories of individuals to whom states must provide coverage under the federal Medicaid program

Causal relationship: A type of relationship in which one factor results in a change in another factor (cause and effect)

Causal-comparative research: A research design that resembles experimental research but lacks random assignment to a group and manipulation of treatment; *See* **quasi experimental design**

Cause-specific death rate: The total number of deaths due to a specific illness during a given time period divided by the estimated population for the same time period

CC: *See* **complications/comorbidities**

CCI: *See* **Correct Coding Initiative**

CCOW: *See* **Clinical Context Object Workgroup**

CCS: *See* **certified coding specialist**

CCS-P: *See* **certified coding specialist-physician based**

CCU: *See* **coronary care unit**

CDACs: *See* **Clinical Data Abstraction Centers**

CDC: *See* **Centers for Disease Control and Prevention**

CDHP: *See* **consumer-directed (driven) healthcare plan**

CDM: *See* **charge description master**

CDR: *See* **clinical data repository**

CDSS: *See* **clinical decision support system**

CDT: *See* **Current Dental Terminology**

CEN: *See* **European Committee for Standardization**

Census: The number of inpatients present in a healthcare facility at any given time

Census-reporting policy: A policy that outlines the process for census reporting and tracking

Census statistics: Statistics that examine the number of patients being treated at specific times, the length of their stay, and the number of times a bed changes occupants

Census survey: A survey that collects data from all the members of a population

Centers for Disease Control and Prevention (CDC): A group of federal agencies that oversee health promotion and disease control and prevention activities in the United States

Centers for Medicare and Medicaid Services (CMS): The division of the Department of Health and Human Services that is responsible for developing healthcare policy in the United States and for administering the Medicare program and the federal portion of the Medicaid program; called the Health Care Financing Administration (HCFA) prior to 2001

Central data repository: *See* **data repository**

CEO: *See* **chief executive officer**

Certainty factor: The defined certainty percentage rate with which an occurrence must present itself to satisfy quality standards

Certificate authority (CA): An independent licensing agency that vouches for a person's identity in encrypted electronic communications

Certificate holder: Member of a group for which an employer or association has purchased group healthcare insurance *See* **insured**, **member**, **policyholder**, and **subscriber**

Certificate of destruction: A document that constitutes proof that a health record was destroyed and that includes the method of destruction, the signature of the person responsible for destruction, and inclusive dates for destruction

Certificate of need (CON): A state-directed program that requires healthcare facilities to submit detailed plans and justifications for the purchase of new equipment, new buildings, or new service offerings that cost in excess of a certain amount

Certification: 1. The process by which a duly authorized body evaluates and recognizes an individual, institution, or educational program as meeting predetermined requirements   2. An evaluation performed to establish the extent to which a particular computer system, network design, or application implementation meets a pre-specified set of requirements

Certification/recertification: Medicare requirement for the physician's official recognition of skilled nursing care needs for the resident

Certification standards: Detailed compulsory requirements for participation in Medicare and Medicaid programs

Certified coding specialist (CCS): An AHIMA credential awarded to individuals who have demonstrated skill in classifying medical data from patient records, generally in the hospital setting, by passing a certification examination

Certified coding specialist—physician based (CCS–P) An AHIMA credential awarded to individuals who have demonstrated coding expertise in physician-based settings, such as group practices, by passing a certification examination

Certified medical transcriptionist (CMT): A certification that is granted upon successful completion of an examination

Certified public accountant (CPA): An individual who has achieved specialized expertise in using and managing financial accounting information

Cesarean section rate: The ratio of all cesarean sections to the total number of deliveries, including cesarean sections, during a specified period of time

CF: *See* **national conversation factor**

CFO: *See* **chief financial officer**

CFR: *See* **Code of Federal Regulations**

Chain of command: A hierarchical reporting structure within an organization

Champion: An individual within an organization who believes in an innovation or change and promotes the idea by building financial and political support

CHAMPUS: *See* **Civilian Health and Medical Program-Uniformed Services**

CHAMPVA: *See* **Civilian Health and Medical Program-Veterans Administration**

Change agent: An individual within an organization whose primary responsibility is to facilitate change

Change control: The process of performing an impact analysis and obtaining approval before modifications to the project scope are made

Change drivers: Forces in the external environment of organizations or industries that force organizations or industries to change the way they operate in order to survive

Change management: The formal process of introducing change, getting it adopted, and diffusing it throughout the organization

Charge: Price assigned to a unit of medical or health service, such as a visit to a physician or a day in a hospital; may be unrelated to the actual cost of providing the service; *See* **fee**

Charge code: The numerical identification of a service or supply that links the item to a particular department within the charge description master

Charge description master (CDM): *See* **chargemaster**

Chargemaster: A financial management form that contains information about the organization's charges for the healthcare services it provides to patients; *See* **charge description master (CDM)**

Charges: The dollar amounts actually billed by healthcare facilities for specific services or supplies and owed by patients

Charisma: The ability of a leader to inspire and motivate others to high performance and commitment

Chart: 1. (noun) The health record of a patient 2. (verb) to document information about a patient in a health record; *See* **documentation**

Chart depletion policy: A policy that outlines the documents that can be removed, or depleted, from resident records over time

Charting by exception: A system of health record documentation in which progress notes focus on abnormal events and describe any interventions that were ordered and the patient's response; *See* **focus charting**

Chart order policy: A policy that provides a detailed listing of all documents and defines their order and section location within the health record

Chart tracking: A system that identifies the current location of a record or information

Chart-tracking/requests policy: A policy that outline the way in which charts are signed out of the permanent files and how requests for records are handled

Check digit: A representation of a checksum operation

Checksheet: A tool that permits the systematic recording of observations of a particular phenomenon so that trends or patterns can be identified

Checksum: Digits or bits summed according to arbitrary rules and used to verify the integrity of numerical data

Chief complaint: The principal problem a patient reports to a healthcare provider

Chief executive officer (CEO): The senior manager appointed by a governing board to direct an organization's overall management

Chief financial officer (CFO): The senior manager responsible for the fiscal management of an organization

Chief information officer (CIO): The senior manager responsible for the overall management of information resources in an organization

Chief nursing officer (CNO): The senior manager (usually a registered nurse with advanced education and extensive experience) responsible for administering patient care services

Chief security officer (CSO): The middle manager responsible for overseeing all aspects of an organization's security plan

Children's Health Insurance Program (CHIP): *See* **State Children's Health Insurance Program (SCHIP)**

Child Welfare League of America (CWLA): An association of public and private nonprofit agencies and organizations across the U.S. and Canada devoted to improving life for abused, neglected, and otherwise vulnerable children and young people and their families

CHIME: *See* **College of Health Information Management Executives**

CHIN: *See* **community health information network**

CHIP: *See* **Children's Health Insurance Program**

CIO: *See* **chief information officer**

Cipher text: A text message that has been encrypted, or converted into code, to make it unreadable in order to conceal its meaning

Circuit switching: Communications technology that establishes a connection between callers in a telephone network using a dedicated circuit path

CIS: *See* **clinical information system**

Civilian Health and Medical Program—Uniformed Services (CHAMPUS): A federal program providing supplementary civilian-sector hospital and medical services beyond that which is available in military treatment facilities to military dependents, retirees and their dependents, and certain others

Civilian Health and Medical Program—Veterans Administration (CHAMPVA): The federal healthcare benefits program for dependents of veterans rated by the Veterans Administration as having a total and permanent disability, for survivors of veterans who died from VA-rated service-connected conditions or who were rated permanently and totally disabled at the time of death from a VA-rated service-connected condition, and for survivors of persons who died in the line of duty

Civil law: The branch of law involving court actions between private parties, corporations, government bodies, or other organizations, typically for the recovery of private rights with compensation usually being monetary

Civil proceeding (action): An action brought to enforce, redress, or protect private rights or to protect a private right or compel a civil remedy in a dispute between private parties (in general, all types of actions other than criminal proceedings)

Civil Rights Act of 1964, Title VII: The federal legislation that prohibits discrimination in employment on the basis of race, religion, color, sex, or national origin

Civil Rights Act of 1991: The federal legislation that focuses on establishing an employer's responsibility for justifying hiring practices that seem to adversely affect people because of race, color, religion, sex, or national origin

Claim: Itemized statement of healthcare services and their costs provided by a hospital, physician's office, or other healthcare provider; submitted for reimbursement to the healthcare insurance plan by either the insured party or by the provider

Claims management: A function related to risk management that enables an organization to track descriptive claims information (incidents, claimants, insurance, demands, dates, and so on), along with data on investigation, litigation, settlement, defendants, and subrogation

Claims processing: The process of accumulating claims for services, submitting claims for reimbursement, and ensuring that claims are satisfied

Class: The higher-level abstraction of an object that defines its properties and operations

Classification system: 1. A system for grouping similar diseases and procedures and organizing related information for easy retrieval   2. A system for assigning numeric or alphanumeric code numbers to represent specific diseases and/or procedures

Clean claim: A claim that has all the billing and coding information correct and can be paid by the payer the first time it is submitted

Client: A patient who receives behavioral or mental health services

Client/server: A computer architecture in which multiple computers (clients) are connected to other computers (servers) that store and distribute large amounts of shared data

Clinic: An outpatient facility providing a limited range of healthcare services and assuming overall healthcare responsibility for patients

Clinical abstract: A computerized file that summarizes patient demographics and other information, including reason for admission, diagnoses, procedures, physician information, and any additional information deemed pertinent by the facility

Clinical algorithm: *See* **care path**

Clinical care plans: Care guidelines created by healthcare providers for individual patients for a specified period of time

Clinical coding: The process of assigning numeric or alphanumeric classifications to diagnostic and procedural statements

Clinical communication space: The context and range of electronic and interpersonal information exchanged among staff and patients

Clinical Context Object Workgroup (CCOW): A standard protocol developed by HL7 to allow clinical applications to share information at the point of care

Clinical data: Data captured during the process of diagnosis and treatment

Clinical Data Abstraction Centers (CDACs): Independent review firms that contract with CMS to perform data collection

Clinical data repository (CDR): A central database that focuses on clinical information

Clinical decision support system (CDSS): A special subcategory of clinical information systems that is designed to help healthcare providers make knowledge-based clinical decisions

Clinical domain: A domain that captures significant indicators of clinical needs from several OASIS items, including patient history, and sensory, integumentary, respiratory, elimination, neurological, emotional, and behavioral status

Clinical drug: A pharmaceutical product given to (or taken by) a patient with a therapeutic or diagnostic intent; has a clinical drug name, which includes the routed generic, the strength, and dose form

Clinical guidelines/protocols: With clinical care plans and clinical pathways, a predetermined method of performing healthcare for a specific disease or other clinical situation based on clinical evidence that the method provides high-quality, cost-effective healthcare; *See* **treatment guidelines/protocols**

Clinical informatics: A field of information science concerned with the management of data and information used to support the practice and delivery of patient care through the application of computers and computer technologies

Clinical information: Health record documentation that describes the patient's condition and course of treatment

Clinical information system (CIS): A category of a healthcare information system that includes systems that directly support patient care

Clinical/medical decision support system: A data-driven decision support system that assists physicians in applying new information to patient care through the analysis of patient-specific clinical/medical variables

Clinical messaging: The function of electronically delivering data and automating the work flow around the management of clinical data

Clinical outcomes system (COS): A data set that provides information on patient outcomes, which is operated by Caredata.com, Inc.

Clinical pathway: A tool designed to coordinate multidisciplinary care planning for specific diagnoses and treatments; *See* **critical path** and **Care Map**

Clinical pertinence review: A review of medical records performed to assess the quality of information using criteria determined by the healthcare organization

Clinical practice guideline: A detailed, step-by-step guide used by healthcare practitioners to make knowledge-based decisions related to patient care and issued by an authoritative organization such as a medical society or government agency; *See* **clinical protocol**

Clinical privileges: The authorization granted by a healthcare organization's governing board to a member of the medical staff that enables the physician to provide patient services in the organization within specific practice limits

Clinical protocol: Specific instructions for performing clinical procedures established by authoritative bodies, such as medical staff committees, and intended to be applied literally and universally; *See* **clinical practice guideline**

Clinical quality assessment: The process for determining whether the services provided to patients meet predetermined standards of care

Clinical repository: A frequently updated database that provides users with direct access to detailed patient-level data as well as the ability to drill down into historical views of administrative, clinical, and financial data; *See* **data warehouse**

Clinical research: A specialized area of research that primarily investigates the efficacy of preventive, diagnostic, and therapeutic procedures; *See* **medical research**

Clinical service: A general term used to indicate a unit of medical staff responsibility (such as cardiology), a unit of inpatient beds (such as general medicine), or even a group of discharged patients with related diseases or treatment (such as orthopedic)

Clinical terminology: A set of standardized terms and their synonyms that can be mapped to broader classifications; *See* **nomenclature**

Clinical Terms, Version 3 (CTV3): A crown copyright work of the National Health Service in the United Kingdom, formerly known as the Read Codes, introduced in the 1980s to facilitate the exchange retrieval and analysis of key data in the medical record; similar to SNOMED; *See* **Read codes**

Clinical trial: A controlled research study involving human subjects that is designed to evaluate prospectively the safety and effectiveness of new drugs, tests, devices, or interventions

Clinical vocabulary: A formally recognized list of preferred medical terms; *See* **medical vocabulary**

Clinical workstation: A single point of access that includes a common user interface to view information from disparate applications and to launch applications

Clinic cases: Patient encounters that take place on an outpatient basis in a clinic within a teaching environment

Clinician: A healthcare provider, including physicians and others who treat patients

Clinician/physician portals: The media for providing physician/clinician access to the provider organization's multiple sources of data from any network-connected device

Clinic outpatient: A patient who is admitted to a clinical service of a clinic or hospital for diagnosis or treatment on an ambulatory basis

Clinic referral: *See* **source of admission**

Clinic without walls (CWW): *See* **group practice without walls**

Closed-ended question: *See* **structured question**

Closed panel: Type of health maintenance organization that provides hospitalization and physicians' services through its own staff and facilities; beneficiaries are allowed to use only those specified facilities and physicians or dentists who accept the plan or organization's conditions of membership and reimbursement; *See* **staff model health maintenance organization** and **group model**

Closed-record review: A review of records after a patient has been discharged from the organization or treatment has been terminated

Closed records: The records of patients who have been discharged from the hospital or whose treatment has been terminated

Closed systems: Systems that operate in a self-contained environment

Cluster sampling: The process of selecting subjects for a sample from each cluster within a population (for example, a family, school, or community)

CMS: *See* **Centers for Medicare and Medicaid Services**

CMS-1500: A Medicare claim form used to bill third-party payers for provider services, for example, physician office visits

CMS-485: A Medicare form used to document care plans

CMS-1450: A Medicare form used for standardized uniform billing

CMT: *See* **certified medical transcriptionist**

CNO: *See* **chief nursing officer**

COA: *See* **Council on Accreditation for Children and Family Services**

Coaching: 1. A training method in which an experienced person gives advice to a less-experienced worker on a formal or informal basis 2. A disciplinary method used as the first step for employees who are not meeting performance expectations

Coalition building: A technique used to manage the political dimensions of change within an organization by building the support of groups for change

COB: *See* **coordination of benefits**

COB transaction: *See* **coordination of benefits transaction**

COBRA: *See* **Consolidated Omnibus Budget Reconciliation Act of 1975**

Code: In information systems, software instructions that direct computers to perform a specified action; in healthcare, an alphanumeric representation of the terms in a clinical classification or vocabulary

Coded data: Data that are translated into a standard nomenclature of classification so that they may be aggregated, analyzed, and compared

Code editor: Software that evaluates the clinical consistency and completeness of health record information and identifies potential errors that could affect accurate prospective payment group assignment

Code look-up: A computer file with all of the indexes and codes recorded on magnetic disk or CD-ROM

Code of Federal Regulations (CFR): The official collection of legislative and regulatory guidelines that are mandated by final rules published in the *Federal Register*

Coder: A person assigned solely to the function of coding

Coder/biller: A person in an ambulatory care or a physician office setting who is generally responsible for processing the superbill

Coding: The process of assigning numeric representations to clinical documentation

Coding Clinic: A publication issued quarterly by the American Hospital Association and approved by the Centers for Medicare and Medicaid Services to give coding advice and direction for ICD-9-CM

Coding formalization principles: A set of principles referring to the transition of coding from analysis of records to a process that involves data analysis using more sophisticated tools (for example, algorithmic translation, concept representation, or vocabulary or reimbursement mapping)

Coding specialist: The healthcare worker responsible for assigning numeric or alphanumeric codes to diagnostic or procedural statements

Cohort study: A study, followed over time, in which a group of subjects is identified as having one or more characteristics in common

Coinsurance: Cost-sharing in which the policy or certificate holder pays a pre-established percentage of eligible expenses after the deductible has been met

COLD/ERM: *See* **Computer Output Laser Disk/Enterprise Report Management**

Collaborative Stage Data Set: A new standardized neoplasm staging system developed by the American Joint Commission on Cancer

Collection: The part of the billing process in which payment for services performed is obtained

College of American Pathologists (CAP): A medical specialty organization of board-certified pathologists; owns and holds the copyright to SNOMED

College of Healthcare Information Management Executives (CHIME): A membership association serving chief information officers through professional development and advocacy

Column/field: A basic fact within a table, such as LAST_ NAME, FIRST_NAME, and date of birth

COMB-1 form: *See* **Attending Physician Statement**

Commission on Accreditation of Rehabilitation Facilities (CARF): A private, not-for-profit organization that develops customer-focused standards for behavioral healthcare and medical rehabilitation programs and accredits such programs on the basis of its standards

Commodity: An article of trade or commerce; especially a product that is essentially the same from one vendor to another

Common-cause variation: The source of variation in a process that is inherent within the process

Common law: Unwritten law originating from court decisions where no applicable statute exists; *See* **judge-made law** or **case law**

Common Object Request Broker Architecture (CORBA): A component computer technology developed by a large consortium of vendors and users for handling objects over a network from various distributed platforms; the subset of standards for healthcare covered in CORBAmed

Communication standards: *See* **transmission standards**

Communications: The manner in which various individual computer systems are connected (for example, telephone lines, microwave, satellite)

Communications plan: A documented approach to identifying the media and schedule for sharing information with affected parties

Community-acquired infection: An infectious disease contracted as the result of exposure before or after a patient's period of hospitalization

Community (-based premium) rating: Method of determining healthcare premium rates by geographic area (community) rather than by age, health status, or company size, which increases the size of the risk pool resulting in increased costs to younger, healthier individuals who are, in effect, subsidizing older or less healthy individuals

Community health information network (CHIN): An integrated collection of computer and telecommunications capabilities that facilitates communications of patient, clinical, and payment information among multiple providers, payers, employers, and related healthcare entities within a community; *See* **community health management information system**

Community health management information system: *See* **community health information network**

Community of Practice (CoP): A Web-based electronic network for communication among members of the American Health Information Management Association

Comorbidity: A medical condition that coexists with the primary cause for hospitalization and affects the patient's treatment and length of stay

Compensable factor: A characteristic used to compare the worth of jobs (for example, skill, effort, responsibility, and working conditions)

Competencies: Demonstrated skills that a worker should perform at a high level

Compiler: 1. A type of software that looks at an entire high-level program before translating it into machine language   2. A third-generation programming language

Complaint: A written legal statement from a plaintiff that initiates a civil lawsuit

Compliance: 1. The process of establishing an organizational culture that promotes the prevention, detection, and resolution of instances of conduct that do not conform to federal, state, or private payer healthcare program requirements or the healthcare organization's ethical and business policies   2. The act of adhering to official requirements

Compliance plan: A process that helps an organization, such as a hospital, accomplish its goal of providing high-quality medical care and efficiently operating a business under various laws and regulations

Compliance program guidance: The information provided by the Office of the Inspector General of the Department of Health and Human Services to help healthcare organizations develop internal controls that promote adherence to applicable federal and state guidelines

Complication: A medical condition that arises during an inpatient hospitalization (for example, a postoperative wound infection)

Complications/comorbidities (CC): Illnesses or injuries that coexist with the condition for which the patient is primarily seeking healthcare

Component alignment model (CAM): A model for strategic information systems planning that includes seven major interdependent components that should be aligned with other components in the organization

Components: Self-contained miniapplications that are an outgrowth of objected-oriented computer programming and provide an easy way to expand, modernize, or customize large-scale applications because they are reusable and less prone to bugs

Comprehensive Drug Abuse Prevention and Control Act of 1970: *See* **Controlled Substances Act**

Comprehensive outpatient program: An outpatient program for the prevention, diagnosis, and treatment of any illness, defect, or condition that prevents the individual from functioning in an optimal manner

Compressed workweek: A work schedule that permits a full-time job to be completed in less than the standard five days of eight-hour shifts

Compression algorithm: The process or program for reducing a message without significantly losing information

Computer-assisted coding: *See* **autocoding**

Computer-based health record: *See* **electronic health record**

Computer-based patient record (CPR): An electronic patient record housed in a system designed to provide users with access to complete and accurate data, practitioner alerts and reminders, clinical decision support systems, and links to medical knowledge; *See* **electronic health record** and **computerized patient record**

Computer-based Patient Record Institute (CPRI): A private organization founded in 1992 to develop a strategy to support the development and adoption of computer-based patient records

Computer-based training: A type of training that is delivered partially or completely using a computer

Computer incident response team: A team organized to investigate and resolve reportable security incidents

Computerized patient record: *See* **computer-based patient record**

Computer Output Laser Disk/Enterprise Report Management (COLD/ERM) technology: Technology that electronically stores the documents and distributes them with fax, email, Web, and traditional hardcopy print processes

Computer–telephone integration (CTI): An integration of computer technology and public telephone services that allows people to access common computer functions such as database queries via telephone handsets or interactive voice technology

Computer telephony: A combination of computer and telephone technologies that allows people to use a telephone handset to access information stored in a computer system or to use computer technology to place calls within the public telephone network

Computer virus: A software program that attacks computer systems and sometimes damages or destroys files

CON: *See* **certificate of need**

Concept: A unit of knowledge or thought created by a unique combination of characteristics

Conceptual data model: The highest level of data model, representing the highest level of abstraction, independent of hardware and software

Conceptual framework of accounting: The concept that the benefits of financial data should exceed the cost of obtaining them and that the data must be understandable, relevant, reliable, and comparable

Concept orientation: Concepts in a controlled medical terminology are based on meanings, not words

Concept permanence: Codes that represent the concept in a controlled medical terminology are not reused; therefore meanings do not change

Conceptual skills: One of the three managerial skill categories that includes intellectual tasks and abilities such as planning, deciding, and problem solving

Concept Unique Identifier (CUI): A numeric identifier in RxNorm that designates the same concept, no matter the form of the name or the table where it is found

Concurrent analysis: A review of the health record while the patient is still hospitalized or under treatment; *See* **concurrent review**

Concurrent coding: A type of coding that takes place while the patient is still in the hospital and receiving care

Concurrent conditions: The physical disorders present at the same time as the primary diagnosis that alter the course of the treatment required or lengthen the expected recovery time of the primary condition

Concurrent review: *See* **concurrent analysis**

Concurrent utilization review: An evaluation of the medical necessity, quality, and cost-effectiveness of a hospital admission and ongoing patient care at or during the time that services are rendered

Conditions of Participation: The administrative and operational guidelines and regulations under which facilities are allowed to take part in the Medicare and Medicaid programs; published by the Centers for Medicare and Medicaid Services, a federal agency under the Department of Health and Human Services

Confidentiality: A legal and ethical concept that establishes the healthcare provider's responsibility for protecting health records and other personal and private information from unauthorized use or disclosure

Confidentiality policy: A policy that outlines the steps to take organizationwide to protect information about residents and the facility from unwanted disclosure

Confounding variable: An event or a factor that is outside a study but occurs concurrently with the study; *See* **extraneous variable** and **secondary variable**

Connectivity: The ability of one computer system to exchange meaningful data with another computer system

Consent: A means for residents to convey to healthcare providers their implied or expressed permission to administer care or treatment or to perform surgery or other medical procedures

Consent to restrain: A consent that is used in instances when the resident must be restrained to ensure quality of life

Consent to treatment: Legal permission given by a patient or a patient's legal representative to a healthcare provider that allows the provider to administer care and/or treatment or to perform surgery and/or other medical procedures

Consent to use and disclose information: A written statement of permission given by a patient to a healthcare provider that allows the provider to use or disclose healthcare information for the purposes of treatment, payment, and healthcare operations

Conservatism: The concept that resources must not be overstated and liabilities not understated

Consideration: The leadership orientation of having concern for people and providing support

Consistency: The idea that all time periods must reflect the same accounting rules

Consolidated billing/bundling: A feature of the prospective payment system established by the Balanced Budget Act of 1997 for home health services provided to Medicare beneficiaries that requires the home health provider that developed the patient's plan of care to assume Medicare billing responsibility for all of the home health services the patient receives to carry out the plan

Consolidated Omnibus Budget Reconciliation Act of 1975 (COBRA): The federal law requiring every hospital that participates in Medicare and has an emergency room to treat any patient in an emergency condition or active labor, whether or not the patient is covered by Medicare and regardless of the patient's ability to pay; COBRA also requires employers to provide continuation benefits to specified workers and families who have been terminated but previously had healthcare insurance benefits

Consolidation: The process by which the ambulatory patient group classification system determines whether separate payment is appropriate when a patient is assigned multiple significant procedure groups

Construct validity: The ability of an instrument to measure hypothetical, nonobservable traits

Consultation: The response by one healthcare professional to another healthcare professional's request to provide recommendations and/or opinions regarding the care of a particular patient/resident

Consultation rate: The total number of hospital inpatients receiving consultations for a given period divided by the total number of discharges and deaths for the same period

Consultation reports: Health record documentation that describes the findings and recommendations of consulting physicians

Consulting agencies: Companies outside the healthcare organization that provide assistance with various issues, including security awareness training

Consumer: A person who purchases and/or uses goods or services; in healthcare, a patient, client, resident, or other recipient of healthcare services

Consumer-directed (driven) healthcare plan (CDHP): Managed care organization characterized by influencing patients and clients to select cost-efficient healthcare through the provision of information about health benefit packages and through financial incentives

Consumer informatics: The field of information science concerned with the management of data and information used to support consumers by consumers (the general public) through the application of computers and computer technologies

Content: The substantive or meaningful components of a document or collection of documents

Content analysis: A method of research that provides a systematic and objective analysis of communication effectiveness, such as the analysis performed on tests

Content validity: The extent to which an instrument's items represent the content that the instrument is intended to measure

Context: The text that illustrates a concept or the use of a designation

Context-based access control: An access control system in which access decisions are based on the conditions (for example, location or time) under which the data are being accessed

Contextual: The condition of depending on the parts of a written or spoken statement that precede or follow a specified word or phrase and can influence its meaning or effect

Contingency: A plan of action to be taken when circumstances affect project performance

Contingency model of leadership: A leadership theory based on the idea that the success of task- or relationship-oriented leadership depends on leader–member relationships, task structure, and position power

Contingency plan: Documentation of the process for responding to a system emergency, including the performance of backups, the preparation of critical facilities that can be used to facilitate continuity of operations in the event of an emergency, and the process of recovering from a disaster

Continued-stay utilization review: A periodic review conducted during a hospital stay to determine whether the patient continues to need acute care services

Continuing care retirement community: An organization established to provide housing and services, including healthcare, to people of retirement age

Continuing education: A type of training that enables employees to remain current in the knowledge base of their profession

Continuous data: Data that represent measurable quantities but are not restricted to certain specified values

Continuous quality improvement (CQI): 1. A management philosophy that emphasizes the importance of knowing and meeting customer expectations, reducing variation within processes, and relying on data to build knowledge for process improvement 2. A continuous cycle of planning, measuring, and monitoring performance and making knowledge-based improvements

Continuous speech recognition: A computer technology that automatically translates voice patterns into written language in real time

Continuous speech technology: A method of encoding speech signals that do not require speaker pauses (but uses pauses when they are present) and of interpreting at least some of the signals' content as words or the intent of the speaker; *See* **voice recognition technology**

Continuum of care: The range of healthcare services provided to patients, from routine ambulatory care to intensive acute care

Contract: A legally enforceable agreement

Contract coder: A coder who is hired on a temporary basis to work on site

Contracted discount rate: A type of fee-for-service reimbursement in which the third party payer has negotiated a reduced ("discounted") fee for its covered parties; *See* **discounted fee-for-service**

Contract law: A branch of law based on common law that deals with written or oral agreements that are enforceable through the legal system

Contract service: An entity that provides certain agreed-upon services for the facility, such as transcription, coding, or copying

Contractual allowance: The difference between what is charged by the healthcare provider and what is paid by the managed care company or other payer

Control: One of the four management functions in which performance is monitored in accordance with organizational policies and procedures

Control chart: A run chart with lines on it called control limits that provides information to help predict the future outcome of a process with a high degree of accuracy

Control group: A comparison study group whose members do not undergo the treatment under study

Controllable costs: Costs that can be influenced by a department director or manager

Controlled medical terminology: A coded vocabulary of medical concepts and expressions used in healthcare

Controlled Substances Act: The legislation that controls the use of narcotics, depressants, stimulants, and hallucinogens; *See* **Comprehensive Drug Abuse Prevention and Control Act of 1970**

Controlled vocabulary: A predefined set of terms and their meanings that may be used in structured data entry or natural language processing to represent expressions

Controls: Subjects used for comparison who are not given a treatment under study or do not have the condition or risk factor that is the object of study

Convenience sample: A type of nonrandom sampling in which researchers use any unit at hand

Conversion factor: A monetary multiplier that converts relative value units into payments

Cookie: A piece of information passed from a Web server to the user's Web browser that is accessible only to the server/domain that sent it and is retrieved automatically through a program called an intelligent agent whenever the server's Web page is visited; used to store passwords and ordering information and to set preferences and bookmarks

Cooperating parties for ICD-9-CM: A group of organizations (the American Health Information Management Association, the American Hospital Association, the Centers for Medicare and Medicaid Services, and the National Center for Health Statistics) that collaborates in the development and maintenance of the *International Classification of Diseases, Ninth Revision, Clinical Modification* (ICD-9-CM)

Coordinated care plans: Organized patient care plans that meet the standards set forth in the law for managed care plans (for example, health maintenance organizations, provider-sponsored organizations, and preferred provider organizations)

Coordination of benefits (COB): A method of integrating benefits payments from all health insurance sources to ensure that they do not exceed 100 percent of a plan member's allowable medical expenses

Coordination of benefits (COB) transaction: The electronic transmission of claims and/or payment information from a healthcare provider to a health plan for the purpose of determining relative payment responsibilities

CoP: *See* **Community of Practice**

COP: *See* **Medicare** *Conditions of Participation*

Copayment: A type of cost sharing arrangement in which the insured pays a fixed out-of-pocket amount for healthcare services

CORBA: *See* **Common Object Request Broker Architecture**

Core communications: A series of triggered, event-specific communications based on need and data such as age, sex, and health profile that gives providers an appropriate time and personalized reason to communicate with recipients

Core measure/core measure set: Standardized performance measures developed to improve the safety and quality of healthcare (for example, core measures are used in the Joint Commission on Accreditation's ORYX initiative)

Coronary care unit (CCU): A facility dedicated to the care of patients who suffer from heart attacks, strokes, or other serious cardiopulmonary problems

Corporate compliance program: A facilitywide program that comprises a system of policies, procedures, and guidelines that are used to ensure ethical business practices

Corporate negligence: The failure of an organization to exercise the degree of care considered reasonable under the circumstances that resulted in an unintended injury to another party

Corporation: An organization that may have one or many owners in which profits may be held or distributed as dividends (income paid to the owners)

Correct Coding Initiative (CCI): A national initiative designed to improve the accuracy of Part B claims processed by Medicare carriers

Correction, addendum, and appending health records policy: A policy that outlines how corrections, addenda, or appendages are made in the resident's health record

Corrective action plan (CAP): A written plan of actions to be taken in response to identified issues or citations from an accrediting or licensing body

Corrective controls: Internal controls designed to fix problems that have been discovered, frequently as a result of detective controls

Correlational research: A design of research that determines the existence and degree of relationships among factors

COS: *See* **clinical outcomes system**

Cost: The dollar amount of a service provided by a facility

Cost allocation: The distribution of costs

Cost–benefit analysis: A process that uses quantitative techniques to evaluate and measure the benefit of providing products or services compared to the cost of providing them

Cost centers: Groups of activities for which costs are specified together for management purposes

Cost driver: An activity that affects or causes costs

Cost inlier: A case in which the cost of treatment falls within the established cost boundaries of the assigned ambulatory patient group payment

Cost justification: A rationale developed to support competing requests for limited resources

Cost object: A product, process, department, or activity for which a healthcare organization wishes to estimate the cost

Cost of capital: The rate of return required to undertake a project

Cost outlier: Exceptionally high costs associated with inpatient care when compared with other cases in the same diagnosis-related group

Cost outlier adjustment: Additional reimbursement for certain high-cost home care cases based on the loss-sharing ratio of costs in excess of a threshold amount for each home health resource group

Cost report: A report that analyzes the direct and indirect costs of providing care to Medicare patients

Cost-sharing: Provision of a healthcare insurance policy that requires policyholders to pay for a portion of their healthcare services; a cost-control mechanism

Council on Accreditation for Children and Family Services (COA): A private not-for-profit organization that accredits child and family service programs using pre-established standards and criteria

Counseling: For CPT purposes, counseling is defined as being a discussion of one or more of the following topics: diagnostic results and impressions, prognosis, risks and benefits of management, instruction for management, importance of compliance, risk factor reduction, and patient and family education

Court/law enforcement referral: *See* **source of admission**

Court of Appeals: A branch of the federal court system that has the power to hear appeals on the final judgments of district courts

Court order: An official direction issued by a court judge and requiring or forbidding specific parties to perform specific actions

Court-ordered warrant (bench warrant): An authorization issued by a court for the attachment or arrest of a person either in the case of contempt or where an indictment has been found or to bring in a witness who does not obey a subpoena

Covered condition: Health condition, illness, injury, disease, or symptom for which the healthcare insurance company will pay

Covered entity: According to the HIPAA privacy rule, any health plan, healthcare clearinghouse, or healthcare provider that transmits specific healthcare transactions in electronic form

Covered expenses: The specific healthcare charges that an insurer will consider for payment under the terms of a health insurance policy; *See* **benefit**

CPA: *See* **certified public accountant**

CPR: *See* **computer-based patient record**

CPR charge payment method: *See* **customary, prevailing and reasonable charge payment method**

CPRI: *See* **Computer-based Patient Record Institute**

CPT: *See* ***Current Procedural Terminology, Fourth Edition***

CQI: *See* **continuous quality improvement**

Cracker: *See* **hacker**

Credential verification organization (CVO): An organization that verifies healthcare professionals' background, licensing, and schooling, and tracks continuing education and other performance measures

Credentialing: The process of reviewing and validating the qualifications (degrees, licenses, and other credentials), of physicians and other licensed independent practitioners, for granting medical staff membership to provide patient care services

Creditable coverage: Prior healthcare coverage that is taken into account to determine the allowable length of preexisting condition exclusion periods (for individuals entering group health plan coverage); includes healthcare insurance through a group health plan or health maintenance organization (HMO), federal employees health benefits program, military healthcare plan (TRICARE), Indian Health Service, state high risk pools, Medicare, Medicaid, coverage under the Consolidated Omnibus Budget Reconciliation Act (COBRA), or other public health plan, but excludes accidental death and dismemberment plan, automobile medical payment insurance, disability insurance, and workers' compensation

Credited coverage: Reduction of waiting period for preexisting condition based on previous creditable coverage (with a lapse in coverage that does not exceed 63 days); may be calculated on a day-by-day basis or other method that is at least as favorable to the individual

Credits: The amounts on the right side of a journal entry

Criminal law: A branch of law that addresses crimes that are wrongful acts against public health, safety, and welfare, usually punishable by imprisonment and/or fine

Criminal proceeding: An action instituted and conducted for the purpose of preventing the commission of a crime or for fixing the guilt of a crime already committed and punishing the offender

Critic: A role in organizational innovation in which an idea is challenged, compared to stringent criteria, and tested against reality

Critical access hospitals: Hospitals that are excluded from the outpatient prospective payment system because they are paid under a reasonable cost-based system as required under section 1834(g) of the Social Security Act

Critical path: The sequence of tasks that determine the project finish date; *See* **clinical pathway** and **Care Map**

CRM: *See* **customer relationship management**

Cross-sectional study: A biomedical research study in which both the exposure and the disease outcome are determined at the same time in each subject; *See* **prevalence study**

Cross-training: The training to learn a job other than the employee's primary responsibility

Crosswalks: Lists of translating codes from one system to another

Crude birth rate: The number of live births divided by the population at risk

Crude death rate: The total number of deaths in a given population for a given period of time divided by the estimated population for the same period of time

Cryptography: The art of keeping data secret through the use of mathematical or logical functions that transform intelligible data into seemingly unintelligible data and back again

CSO: *See* **chief security officer**

CTI: *See* **computer-telephone integration**

CTV3: *See* **Clinical Terms, Version 3**

CUI: *See* **Concept Unique identifier**

Cultural competence: Skilled in awareness, understanding, and acceptance of beliefs and values of the people of groups other than one's own

Current assets: Cash and other assets that typically will be converted to cash within 1 year

Current Dental Terminology (CDT): A medical code set of dental procedures, maintained and copyrighted by the American Dental Association (ADA), referred to as the Uniform Code on Dental Procedures and Nomenclatures until 1990

***Current Procedural Terminology, Fourth Edition* (CPT):** A comprehensive, descriptive list of terms and numeric codes used for reporting diagnostic and therapeutic procedures and other medical services performed by physicians; published and updated annually by the American Medical Association

Current ratio: The total current assets divided by total current liabilities

Curriculum: A prescribed course of study in an educational program

Custodial care: A type of care that is not directed toward a cure or restoration to a previous state of health but includes medical or nonmedical services provided to maintain a given level of health without skilled nursing care

Customary, prevailing and reasonable (CPR) charge payment method: Type of retrospective fee-for-service payment method, used by Medicare until 1992 to determine payment amounts for physician services, in which the third party payer pays for fees that are customary, prevailing, and reasonable

Customer: An internal or external recipient of services, products, or information

Customer relationship management (CRM): A management system whereby organizational structure and culture and customer information and technology are aligned with business strategy so that all customer interactions can be conducted to the long-term satisfaction of the customer and to the benefit and profit of the organization

CVO: *See* **credential verification organization**

CWLA: *See* **Child Welfare League of America**

CWW: *See* **clinic without walls**

Cybernetic systems: Systems that have standards, controls, and feedback mechanisms built in to them

Cyclical staffing: A transitional staffing solution wherein workers are brought in for specific projects or to cover in busy times

Daily census: The number of inpatients present at the census-taking time each day, plus any inpatients who were both admitted after the previous census-taking time and discharged before the next census-taking time

Daily inpatient census: The number of inpatients present at census-taking time each day, plus any inpatients who were both admitted and discharged after the census-taking time the previous day

Damaged record recovery policy: A policy that outlines the steps the facility should take to recover paper and/or electronic records in the event of a disaster

Data: The dates, numbers, images, symbols, letters, and words that represent basic facts and observations about people, processes, measurements, and conditions

Data accessibility: The extent to which healthcare data are obtainable

Data accuracy: The extent to which data are free of identifiable errors

Data administrator: An emerging role responsible for managing the less technical aspects of data, including data quality and security

Data analysis: The process of translating data into information that can be used by an application

Data availability: The extent to which healthcare data are accessible whenever and wherever they are needed

Data backup plan: A plan that ensures the recovery of information that is lost or becomes inaccessible

Database: An organized collection of data, text, references, or pictures in a standardized format, typically stored in a computer system for multiple applications

Database administrator: The individual responsible for the technical aspects of designing and managing databases

Database life cycle (DBLC): A system consisting of several phases that represent the useful life of a database, including initial study, design, implementation, testing and evaluation, operation, and maintenance and evaluation

Database management: The process of controlling access to the information in a database that uses passwords or other access control techniques

Database management system (DBMS): Computer software that enables the user to create, modify, delete, and view the data in a database

Database model: A description of the structure to be used to organize data in a healthcare-related database such as a computer-based patient record

Data capture: The process of recording healthcare-related data in a health record system or clinical database

Data collection: The process by which data are gathered

Data comparability: The standardization of vocabulary such that the meaning of a single term is the same each time the term is used in order to produce consistency in information derived from the data

Data comprehensiveness: The extent to which healthcare data are complete

Data confidentiality: The extent to which personal health information is kept private

Data consistency: The extent to which healthcare data are reliable

Data conversion: The task of moving data from one data structure to another, usually at the time of a new system installation

Data cube: A collection of one or more tables of data, assembled in a fashion that allows for dynamic analysis to be conducted on the joins, intersections, and overall integration of these predefined tables

Data currency: The extent to which data are up-to-date; *See* **data timeliness**

Data definition: The specific meaning of a healthcare-related data element

Data definition language (DDL): A special type of software used to create the tables within a relational database, the most common of which is structured query language

Data dictionary: A descriptive list of the data elements to be collected in an information system or database whose purpose is to ensure consistency of terminology

Data display: A method for presenting or viewing data

Data element: An individual fact or measurement that is the smallest unique subset of a database

Data Elements for Emergency Department Systems (DEEDS): A data set designed to support the uniform collection of information in hospital-based emergency departments

Data Encryption Standard (DES): A private key encryption algorithm adopted as the federal standard for the protection of sensitive unclassified information and also used extensively for the protection of commercial data

Data exchange standards: Protocols that help ensure that data transmitted from one system to another remain comparable

Data field: An area within a healthcare database in which the same type of information is usually recorded

Data granularity: The level of detail at which the attributes and values of healthcare data are described

Data input: The process of entering data into a healthcare database

Data integrity: 1. The extent to which healthcare data are complete, accurate, consistent, and timely   2. A security principle that keeps information from being modified or otherwise corrupted either maliciously or accidentally

Data manipulation language (DML): A special type of software used to retrieve, update, and edit data in a relational database, of which the most common is structured query language

Data mart: A well-organized, user-centered, searchable database system that usually draws information from a data warehouse to meet the specific needs of users

Data mining: The process of extracting information from a database and then quantifying and filtering discrete, structured data

Data model: A picture or abstraction of real conditions used to design the definitions of fields and records and their relationships in a database

Data modeling: The process of determining the users' information needs and identifying relationships among the data

Data precision: The extent to which data have values that they are expected to have

Data quality management: A managerial process that ensures the integrity (accuracy and completeness) of an organization's data during data collection, application, warehousing, and analysis

Data quality review: An examination of health records to determine the level of coding accuracy and to identify areas of coding problems

Data relevancy: The extent to which healthcare-related data are useful for the purpose for which they were collected

Data reliability: The stability, repeatability, or precision of data

Data repository: An open-structure database that is not dedicated to the software of any particular vendor or data supplier, in which data from diverse sources are stored so that an integrated, multidisciplinary view of the data can be achieved; also called a central data repository or, when related specifically to healthcare data, a clinical data repository

Data resource manager: A role that ensures that the organization's information systems meet the needs of people who provide and manage patient services

Data retrieval: The process of obtaining data from a healthcare database

Data security: The process of keeping data safe from unauthorized alteration or destruction

Data set: A list of recommended data elements with uniform definitions that are relevant for a particular use

Data store: A real-time, sensitive, operationally oriented form of data warehousing, retaining small amounts of key indicators to run day-to-day processes

Data storage: The physical location and maintenance of data

Data structure: The form in which data are stored, as in a file, a database, a data repository, and so on

Data timeliness: *See* **data currency**

Data type: A technical category of data (text, numbers, currency, date, memo, and link data) that a field in a database can contain

Data validity: The extent to which data are verified

Data warehouse: A database that makes it possible to access data from multiple databases and combine the results into a single query and reporting interface; *See* **clinical repository**

Data warehouse management system (DWMS): A type of software that manages a data warehouse

Date of birth: The year, month, and day when an individual was born

Date of encounter: In outpatient and physician services settings, the year, month, and day of an encounter, visit, or other healthcare encounter

Date of procedure: In inpatient settings, the year, month, and day of each significant procedure

Date of service (DOS): The date a test, procedure, and/or service was rendered

Day on leave of absence: A day occurring after the admission and prior to the discharge of a hospital inpatient when the patient is not present at the census-taking hour because he or she is on leave of absence from the healthcare facility

Day outlier: An inpatient hospital stay that is exceptionally long when compared with other cases in the same diagnosis-related group

Days in accounts receivable: The ending accounts receivable balance divided by an average day's revenues

Days of stay: *See* **length of stay**

DBLC: *See* **database life cycle**

DBMS: *See* **database management system**

DDL: *See* **data definition language**

Dead on arrival (DOA): The condition of a patient who arrives at a healthcare facility with no signs of life and who was pronounced dead by a physician

Death rate: The proportion of inpatient hospitalizations that end in death

Debit: The amount on the left side of an account entry that represents an increase in an expense or liability account or a decrease in a revenue or asset account

Debt financing: The process of borrowing money at a cost in the form of interest

Debt ratio: The total liabilities divided by the total assets

Decentralization: The shift of decision-making authority and responsibility to lower levels of the organization

Decision support system (DSS): A computer-based system that gathers data from a variety of sources and assists in providing structure to the data by using various analytical models and visual tools in order to facilitate and improve the ultimate outcome in decision-making tasks associated with nonroutine and nonrepetitive problems

Decision tree: A structured data-mining technique based on a set of rules useful for predicting and classifying information and making decisions

Deductible: The amount of cost, usually annual, that the policyholder must incur before the insurance plan will assume liability for remaining covered expenses

Deductive reasoning: The process of developing conclusions based on generalizations

DEEDS: *See* **Data Elements for Emergency Department Systems**

Deemed status: An official designation indicating that a healthcare facility is in compliance with the Medicare *Conditions of Participation*; to qualify for deemed status, facilities must be accredited by the Joint Commission on Accreditation of Healthcare Organizations or the American Osteopathic Association

Default: The status to which a computer application reverts in the absence of alternative instructions

Default judgment: A court ruling against a defendant in a lawsuit who fails to answer a summons for a court appearance

Defendant: In civil cases, an individual or entity against whom a civil complaint has been filed; in criminal cases, an individual who has been accused of a crime

Deficiency analysis: An audit process designed to ensure that all services billed have been documented in the health record

Deficiency slip: A device for tracking information (for example, reports) missing from a paper-based health record

Deficiency systems: Paper- or computer-based processes designed to track and report elements of documentation missing from the health records of discharged patients

Degaussing: The process of removing or rearranging the magnetic field of a disk in order to render the data unrecoverable

Deidentified information: Health information from which all names and other identifying descriptors have been removed to protect the privacy of the patients, family members, and healthcare providers who were involved in the case

Deidentify: The act of removing from a health record or data set any information that could be used to identify the individual to whom the data apply in order to protect his or her confidentiality

Delegation: The process by which managers distribute work to others along with the authority to make decisions and take action

Delinquent health record: An incomplete record not finished or made complete within the time frame determined by the medical staff of the facility

Deliverable: A tangible output produced by the completion of project tasks

Delivery: The process of delivering a liveborn infant or dead fetus (and placenta) by manual, instrumental, or surgical means

Delivery room: A special operating room for obstetric delivery and infant resuscitation

Delivery system: An organized method of providing healthcare services to a large number of individuals in a geopolitical region or a contractually defined population

Demand bill: A bill generated and issued to the patient at the time of service

Demographic information: Information used to identify an individual, such as name, address, gender, age, and other information linked to a specific person

Denial: The circumstance when a bill has been accepted, but payment has been denied for any of several reasons

(for example, sending the bill to the wrong insurance company, patient not having current coverage, inaccurate coding, lack of medical necessity, and so on)

Dental Codes: A separate category of national codes that list codes for billing for dental procedures and supplies

Dental informatics: A field of information science concerned with the management of data and information used to support the practice and delivery of dental healthcare through the application of computers and computer technologies

Department of a provider: A facility, organization, or physician's office that is either created or acquired by a main provider for the purpose of furnishing healthcare services under the name, ownership, and financial and administrative control of the main provider, in accordance with the provisions of the ambulatory payment classification final rule

Department of Health and Human Services ((D)HHS): The cabinet-level federal agency that oversees all of the health- and human-services–related activities of the federal government and administers federal regulations

Dependency: The relationship between two tasks in a project plan

Dependent: An enrolled health plan member who has coverage tied to that of a sponsor, such as a spouse, same-sex domestic partner, an unmarried child, or a stepchild or legally adopted child of the employee or the employee's spouse

Dependent variable: A measurable variable in a research study that depends on an independent variable

Deposition: A method of gathering information to be used in a litigation process

Depreciation: The allocation of the dollar cost of a capital asset over its expected life

Derived attribute: An attribute whose value is based on the value of other attributes (for example, current date minus date of birth yields the derived attribute age)

DES: *See* **Data Encryption Standard**

Description: In a controlled medical vocabulary, a description is the combination of a concept and a term

Descriptive research: A type of research that determines and reports the current status of topics and subjects

Descriptive statistics: A set of statistical techniques used to describe data such as means, frequency distributions, and standard deviations; statistical information that describes the characteristics of a specific group or a population

Design phase: The second phase of the systems development life cycle during which all options in selecting a new information system are considered

Designated record set: A group of records maintained by or for a covered entity that may include patient medical and billing records; the enrollment, payment, claims adjudication, and cases or medical management record systems maintained by or for a health plan; or information used, in whole or in part, to make patient care-related decisions

Destruction: The act of breaking down the components of a health record into pieces that can no longer be recognized as parts of the original record; for example, paper records can be destroyed by shredding, and electronic records can be destroyed by magnetic degaussing

Detective control: An internal control designed to find errors that have already been made

Development: The process of growing or progressing in one's level of skill, knowledge, or ability

Developmental disability: A mental or physical limitation affecting major life activities, arising before adulthood, and usually lasting throughout life

Device driver: A type of software that controls specific hardware, such as the printer driver that ensures that the computer directs printing instructions appropriate to the type of printer to which it is connected

Diagnosis: A word or phrase used by a physician to identify a disease from which an individual patient suffers or a condition for which the patient needs, seeks, or receives medical care

Diagnosis chiefly responsible for services provided (outpatient): The diagnosis, condition, problem, or reason for an encounter/visit that is chiefly responsible for the services provided

Diagnosis-related group (DRG): A unit of case-mix classification adopted by the federal government and some other payers as a prospective payment mechanism for hospital inpatients in which diseases are placed into groups because related diseases and treatments tend to consume similar amounts of healthcare resources and incur similar amounts of cost; in the Medicare and

Medicaid programs, one of more than 500 diagnostic classifications in which cases demonstrate similar resource consumption and length-of-stay patterns

Diagnostic and Statistical Manual of Mental Disorders, Fourth Revision (DSM-IV): A nomenclature developed by the American Psychiatric Association to standardize the diagnostic process for patients with psychiatric disorders; includes codes that correspond to ICD-9-CM codes

Diagnostic codes: Numeric or alphanumeric characters used to classify and report diseases, conditions, and injuries

Diagnostic criteria: For each mental disorder listed in the DSM-IV, a set of extensive diagnostic criteria is provided that indicate what symptoms must be present as well as those symptoms that must not be present in order for a patient to meet the qualifications for a particular mental diagnosis

Diagnostic image data: Bit-mapped images used for medical or diagnostic purposes (for example, chest x-rays or computed tomography scans)

Diagnostic services: All diagnostic services of any type, including history, physical examination, laboratory, x-ray or radiography, and others that are performed or ordered pertinent to the patient's reasons for the encounter

Dichotomous data: *See* **nominal level data**

DICOM: *See* **Digital Imaging and Communication in Medicine**

Diffusion S curve: The S-shaped curve that describes the initially gradual, then more rapid, and finally plateauing adoption of an innovation

Digital: 1. A data transmission type based on data that have been binary encoded   2. A term that refers to the data or information represented in an encoded, computer-readable format

Digital certificate: An electronic document that establishes a person's online identity

Digital dictation: A process in which vocal sounds are converted to bits and stored on computer for random access

Digital Imaging and Communication in Medicine (DICOM): A standard that promotes a digital image communications format and picture archive and communications systems for use with digital images

Digital signature: An electronic signature that binds a message to a particular individual and can be used by the receiver to authenticate the identity of the sender

Direct costs: Costs that are traceable to a given cost object

Direct medical education costs: An add-on to the ambulatory payment classification amount to compensate for costs associated with outpatient direct medical education of interns and residents

Direct method of allocation: A budgeting concept in which the cost of overhead departments is distributed solely to the revenue-producing areas

Direct obstetric death: The death of a woman resulting from obstetric complications of the pregnancy state, labor, or puerperium; from interventions, omissions, or treatment; or from a chain of events resulting from any of the events listed

Direct relationship: *See* **positive relationship**

Disability: A physical or mental condition that either temporarily or permanently renders a person unable to do the work for which he or she is qualified and educated

Disaster recovery: 1. A plan developed by an organization in anticipation of potential natural and manmade disasters that describes the actions the organization would take to minimize damages and resume operations 2. A written plan that documents the process whereby an organization would restore any loss of electronic data and records in the event of fire, vandalism, natural disaster, or computer system failure

Discharge abstract system: A data repository (usually electronic) used for collecting information on demographics, clinical conditions, and services in which data are condensed from hospital health records into coded data for the purpose of producing summary statistics about discharged patients

Discharge analysis: An analysis of the health record at or following discharge

Discharge and readmit: A situation in which a home health provider receives a prorated partial episode payment for the original episode when a beneficiary is discharged and readmitted to the same agency within the same sixty-day period

Discharge date (inpatient): The year, month, and day that an inpatient was formally released from the hospital and room, board, and continuous nursing services were terminated

Discharge days: *See* **length of stay** and **total length of stay**

Discharge diagnosis: Any one of the diagnoses recorded after all the data accumulated during the course of a patient's hospitalization or other circumscribed episode of medical care have been studied

Discharge diagnosis list: A complete set of discharge diagnoses applicable to a single patient episode, such as an inpatient hospitalization

Discharged, no final bill (DNFB) report: A report that includes all patients who have been discharged from the facility but for whom, for one reason or another, the billing process is not complete

Discharge planning: The process of coordinating the activities related to the release of a patient when inpatient hospital care is no longer needed

Discharge status: The disposition of the patient at discharge (that is, left against medical advice, discharged to home, transferred to skilled nursing facility, or died)

Discharge summary: A summary of the resident's stay at the long-term care facility that is used along with the postdischarge plan of care to provide continuity of care for the resident upon discharge from the facility

Discharge transfer: The transfer of an inpatient to another healthcare institution at the time of discharge

Discharge utilization review: A process for assessing a patient's readiness to leave the hospital

Discipline: A field of study characterized by a knowledge base and perspective that is different from other fields of study

Disclosure: The act of making information known; in the health information management context, the release of confidential health information about an identifiable person to another person or entity

Discounted fee for service: A rate agreed to between the provider and the health plan that is lower than the provider's customary fee; *See* **contracted discount rate**

Discounting: The application of lower rates of payment to multiple surgical procedures performed during the same operative session under the outpatient prospective payment system; the application of adjusted rates of payment by preferred provider organizations

Discovery process: The pretrial stage in the litigation process during which both parties to a suit use various strategies to identify information about the case, the primary focus of which is to determine the strength of the opposing party's case

Discovery request: A petition for discovery

Discrete data: Data that represent separate and distinct values or observations; that is, data that contain only finite numbers and have only specified values

Discrete variable: A dichotomous or nominal variable whose values are placed into categories

Discus monitoring form: *See* **Antipsychotic Dyskinesia Identification System**

Disease index: A list of diseases and conditions of patients sequenced according to the code numbers of the classification system in use

Disease management: A more expansive view of case management in which patients with the highest risk of incurring high-cost interventions are targeted for standardizing and managing care throughout integrated delivery systems   2. A program focused on preventing exacerbations of chronic diseases and on promoting healthier life styles for patients and clients with chronic diseases

Disease registry: A centralized collection of data used to improve the quality of care and measure the effectiveness of a particular aspect of healthcare delivery

Disenrollment: A process of termination of coverage of a plan member

Disk mirroring: The creation of an exact copy of one disk from another, for backup

Disposition: For outpatients, the healthcare practitioner's description of the patient's status at discharge (no follow-up planned; follow-up planned or scheduled; referred elsewhere; expired); for inpatients, a core health data element that identifies the circumstances under which the patient left the hospital (discharged alive; discharged to home or self-care; discharged and transferred to another short-term general hospital for inpatient care; discharged and transferred to a skilled nursing facility; discharged and transferred to an intermediate care facility; discharged and transferred to another type of institution for inpatient care or referred for outpatient services to another institution; discharged and transferred to home under care of organized home health services organization; discharged and transferred to home under care of a home intravenous therapy provider; left against medical advice or discontinued care; expired; status not stated)

Distance learning: A learning delivery mode in which the instructor, the classroom, and the students are not all present in the same location and at the same time

Distribution-free technique: *See* **nonparametric technique**

District court: The lowest tier in the federal court system, which hears cases involving felonies and misdemeanors that fall under federal statute and suits in which a citizen of one state sues a citizen of another state

Diversity: Any perceived difference among people, such as age, functional specialty, profession, sexual orientation, geographic origin, lifestyle, or tenure with the organization or position

Diversity training: A type of training that facilitates an environment that fosters tolerance and appreciation of individual differences within the organization's workforce and strives to create a more harmonious working environment

Divestiture: The result of a parent company selling a portion of the company to an outside party for cash or other assets

Dividends: The portion of an organization's profit that is distributed to its investors

DME: *See* **durable medical equipment**

DMERC: *See* **durable medical equipment regional carrier**

DML: *See* **data manipulation language**

DNFB Report: *See* **discharged, no final bill report**

DNR: *See* **do not resuscitate**

DOA: *See* **dead on arrival**

Document: Any analog or digital, formatted, and preserved "container" of data or information

Documentation: The recording of pertinent healthcare findings, interventions, and responses to treatment as a business record and form of communication among caregivers

Document image data: Bit-mapped images based on data created and/or stored on analog paper or photographic film

Document imaging technology: The practice of electronically scanning written or printed paper documents into an optical or electronic system for later retrieval of the document or parts of the document if parts have been indexed

Document management technology: Technology that organizes/assembles, secures, and shares documents, and includes such functions as document version control, check in-check out control, document access control, and text/word searches

Dollars billed: The amount of money billed for services rendered

Dollars in accounts receivable: The amount of money owed a healthcare facility when claims are pending

Dollars received: Payments agreed on through diagnosis-related group selection, contractual agreements, or other payer payment methods

Do not resuscitate (DNR): An order written by the treating physician stating that in the event the patient suffers cardiac or pulmonary arrest, cardiopulmonary resuscitation should not be attempted

DOS: *See* **date of service**

Dose form: The form in which a drug is administered to a patient, as opposed to the form in which the manufacturer had supplied it

Double-blind study: A type of clinical trial conducted with strict procedures for randomization in which neither researcher nor subject knows whether the subject is in the control group or the experimental group

Double distribution: A budgeting concept in which overhead costs are allocated twice, taking into consideration that some overhead departments provide services to each other

Double-entry accounting: A generally accepted method for recording accounting transactions in which debits are posted in the column on the left and credits are posted in the column on the right

Downsizing: A reengineering strategy to reduce the cost of labor and streamline the organization by laying off portions of the workforce

Downtime procedures for health records policy: A policy that outline the steps the department should take when computerized equipment fails or systems are down

DPAHC: *See* **durable power of attorney for healthcare**

DRG: *See* **diagnosis-related group**

DRG creep: An increase in a case-mix index that occurs through the coding of higher-paying principal diagnoses and of more complications and comorbidities, even though the actual severity level of the patient population did not change

DRG grouper: A computer program that assigns inpatient cases to diagnosis-related groups and determines the Medicare reimbursement rate

Drivers and passengers: The exploding charges wherein the driver is the item that explodes into other items and appears on the bill

Drug components: The elements that together constitute a clinical drug

Drug Listing Act of 1972: This act amended the Federal Food, Drug, and Cosmetic Act so that drug establishments that are engaged in the manufacturing, preparation, propagation, compounding, or processing of a drug are required to register their establishments and list all of their commercially marketed drug products with the Food and Drug Administration (FDA)

DSM-IV: *See* **Diagnostic and Statistical Manual of Mental Disorders, Fourth Revision**

DSM-IV-TR Classification: A listing of psychiatric disorders that includes corresponding ICD-9-CM codes (i.e. 315.31, Expressive Language Disorder)

DSS: *See* **decision support system**

Dual option: The offering of health maintenance organization coverage as well as indemnity insurance by the same carrier

Due diligence: The actions associated with making a good decision, including investigation of legal, technical, human, and financial predictions and ramifications of proposed endeavors with another party

Dumping: The illegal practice of transferring uninsured and indigent patients who need emergency services from one hospital to another (usually public) hospital solely to avoid the cost of providing uncompensated services

Durable medical equipment (DME): Medical equipment designed for long-term use in the home, including eyeglasses, hearing aids, surgical appliances and supplies, orthotics and prostheses, and bulk and cylinder oxygen; *See* **home medical equipment (HME)**

Durable medical equipment regional carrier (DMERC): A fiscal intermediary designated to process claims for durable medical equipment

Durable power of attorney for healthcare (DPAHC): A third party designated by a competent individual to make healthcare decisions for that individual should he or she become incompetent

Duration: The amount of time, usually measured in days, for a task to be completed

Duration of inpatient hospitalization: *See* **length of stay**

DWMS: *See* **data warehouse management system**

Early adopters: A category of adopters of change who are leaders, role models, and opinion leaders

Early majority: A category of adopters of innovations who are not leaders but are deliberate in thinking and building a bridge with later adopters

Earnings report: *See* **statement of revenue and expenses**

E code (external cause of injury code): A supplementary ICD-9-CM classification used to identify the external causes of injuries, poisonings, and adverse effects of pharmaceuticals

e-commerce: The use of the Internet and its derived technologies to integrate all aspects of business-to-business and business-to-consumer activities, processes, and communications

ECRI: An independent nonprofit health services research agency, formerly known as the Emergency Care Research Institute

EDI: *See* **electronic data interchange**

Edit: A condition that must be satisfied before a computer system can accept data

EDMs: *See* **electronic document management systems**

Educational Level: The highest level, in years, within each major (primary, secondary, baccalaureate, postbaccalaureate) educational system, regardless of any certifications achieved

Effectiveness: The degree to which stated outcomes are attained

Efficiency: The degree to which a minimum of resources is used to obtain outcomes

Effort: The mental and physical exertion required to perform job-related tasks

e-forms technology: *See* **automated forms processing technology**

e-health: The application of e-commerce to the healthcare industry, including electronic data interchange and links among healthcare entities

e-HIM: The application of technology to managing health information

EHR: *See* **electronic health record**

EHR Collaborative: A group of healthcare professional and trade associations formed to support Health Level Seven, a healthcare standards development organization, in the development of a functional model for electronic health record systems

Eighty-five/fifteen (85/15) rule: The total quality management assumption that 85 percent of the problems that occur are related to faults in the system rather than to worker performance

EIN: *See* **employer identification number**

EIS: *See* **executive information system**

e-learning: The use of the Internet and its derived technologies to deliver training and education

Elective admission: The formal acceptance by a healthcare organization of a patient whose condition permits adequate time to schedule the availability of a suitable accommodation

Elective surgery: A classification of surgery that does not have to be performed immediately to prevent death or serious disability

Electronic data interchange (EDI): A standard transmission format using strings of data for business information communicated among the computer systems of independent organizations

Electronic document management systems (EDMs): A storage solution based on digital scanning technology in which source documents are scanned to create digital images of the documents that can be stored electronically on optical disks; *See* **document management technology**

Electronic health record (EHR): A computerized record of health information and associated processes; *See* **computer-based patient record** and **computer-based health record**

Electronic medical record (EMR): A form of computer-based health record in which information is stored in whole files instead of by individual data elements

Electronic Performance Support System (EPSS): Sets of computerized tools and displays that automate training, documentation, and phone support; that integrate this automation into applications; and that provide support that is faster, cheaper, and more effective than traditional methods

Electronic records management technology: Systems that create and preserve electronic records

Electronic remittance advice (ERA): A classification of payment information from third-party payers that is communicated electronically

Electronic signature: 1. Any representation of a signature in digital form, including an image of a handwritten signature 2. The authentication of a computer entry in a health record made by the individual making the entry

Eligibility date: The date on which a member of an insured group may apply for insurance

Eligibility period: The period of time following the eligibility date (usually thirty-one days) during which a member of an insured group may apply for insurance without evidence of insurability

ELISA: *See* **enzyme-linked immunosorbent assay**

E/M coding: *See* **evaluation and management codes**

EMDS: *See* **Essential Medical Data Set**

Emergency: A situation in which a patient requires immediate medical intervention as a result of severe, life-threatening, or potentially disabling conditions

Emergency Care Research Institute: *See* **ECRI**

Emergency Maternal and Infant Care Program (EMIC): The federal medical program that provides obstetrical and infant care to dependents of active-duty military personnel in the four lowest pay grades

Emergency mode operation plan: A plan that ensures operational continuity for some period of time and defines how the organization would operate in the event of fire, vandalism, natural disaster, or system failure

Emergency patient: A patient who is admitted to the emergency services department of a hospital for the diagnosis and treatment of a condition that requires immediate medical, dental, or allied health services in order to sustain life or to prevent critical consequences

Emergency services: Immediate evaluation and therapy rendered in urgent clinical conditions and sustained until the patient can be referred to his or her personal practitioner for further care

EMIC: *See* **Emergency Maternal and Infant Care Program**

Emotional intelligence: The sensitivity and ability to monitor and revise one's behavior based on the needs of and responses by others

EMPI: *See* **enterprise master patient index**

Empiricism: The quality of being based on observed and validated evidence

Employee Retirement Income Security Act of 1974 (ERISA): Federal legislation designed to protect the pension rights of employees; also prohibits states from applying certain mandates to self-insured health benefit plans

Employer-based self-insurance: An umbrella term used to describe health plans that are funded directly by employers to provide coverage for their employees exclusively in which employers establish accounts to cover their employees' medical expenses and retain control over the funds but bear the risk of paying claims greater than their estimates

Employer identification number (EIN): The federal tax identification number of a business, designated in HIPAA as the standard identifier for employers

Employment contract: A legal and binding agreement of terms related to an individual's work, such as hours, pay, or benefits

Empowerment: The condition of having the environment and resources to perform a job independently

EMR: *See* **electronic medical record**

Enabling technologies: Any newly developed equipment that facilitates data gathering or information processing not possible previously

Encoder: Specialty software used to facilitate the assignment of diagnostic and procedural codes according to the rules of the coding system

Encounter: The direct personal contact between a patient and a physician or other person who is authorized by state licensure law and, if applicable, by medical staff bylaws to order or furnish healthcare services for the diagnosis or treatment of the patient

Encryption: The process of transforming text into an unintelligible string of characters that can be transmitted via communications media with a high degree of security and then decrypted when it reaches a secure destination

Ending: The first stage of Bridges's model of transition management in which people experience losses because of change

Endorsement: Language or statements within a healthcare insurance policy providing additional details about coverage or lack of coverage for special situations that are not usually included in standard policies; may function as a limitation or exclusion

Enterprise master patient index (EMPI): An index that provides access to multiple repositories of information from overlapping patient populations that are maintained in separate systems and databases

Enterprise resource planning (ERP): The use of software tools to automate tasks and track data generated by specific departments (primarily finance, inventory, and human resources) in order to optimize resource utilization

Entity: An individual person, group, or organization

Entity authentication: The corroboration that an entity is who it claims to be

Entity relationship diagram (ERD): A specific type of data modeling used in conceptual data modeling and the logical-level modeling of relational databases

Environmental assessment: External—a collection of information about changes that have occurred in the healthcare industry as well as the broader U.S. economy during a specified time period; internal—a collection of information about changes that have occurred within an organization during a specified time period

Environmental scanning: A systematic and continuous effort to search for important cues about how the world is changing outside and inside the organization

Enzyme-linked immunosorbent assay (ELISA): A test used to detect the presence of HIV antibody and antigen in both blood and bodily fluids

EOB: *See* **explanation of benefits**

EOC reimbursement: *See* **episode-of-care reimbursement**

EPA: *See* **Equal Pay Act of 1963**

Epidemiological data: Data used to reveal disease trends within a specific population

Epidemiological studies: Studies that are concerned with finding the causes and effects of diseases and conditions

Episode: The sixty-day unit of payment for the home health prospective payment system

Episode of care: A period of relatively continuous medical care performed by healthcare professionals in relation to a particular clinical problem or situation

Episode-of-care (EOC) reimbursement: A category of payments made as lump sums to providers for all healthcare services delivered to a patient for a specific illness and/or over a specified time period; also called **bundled payments** because they include multiple services and may include multiple providers of care

EPO: *See* **exclusive provider organization**

EPSS: *See* **Electronic Performance Support System**

Equal Pay Act of 1963 (EPA): The federal legislation that requires equal pay for men and women who perform substantially the same work

Equity: The difference between assets and liabilities

Equity financing: The retained earnings or profits generated by an organization

ERA: *See* **electronic remittance advice**

ERD: *See* **entity relationship diagram**

Ergonomics: A discipline of functional design associated with the employee in relationship to his or her work environment, including equipment, workstation, and office furniture adaptation to accommodate the employee's unique physical requirements so as to facilitate efficacy of work functions

ERISA: *See* **Employee Retirement Income Security Act of 1974**

ERP: *See* **enterprise resource planning**

Essential Medical Data Set (EMDS): A recommended data set designed to create a health history for an individual patient treated in an emergency service

Established patient: A patient who has received professional services from the physician or another physician of the same specialty in the same practice group within the past three years

Ethical decision making: The process of requiring everyone to consider the perspectives of others, even when they do not agree with them

Ethicist: An individual trained in the application of ethical theories and principles to problems that cannot be easily solved because of conflicting values, perspectives, and options for action

Ethics: A field of study that deals with moral principles, theories, and values; in healthcare, a formal decision-making process for dealing with the competing perspectives and obligations of the people who have an interest in a common problem

Ethnic group: The cultural group with which the patient identifies by means of either recorded family data or personal preference

Ethnicity: A category in the Uniform Hospital Discharge Data Set that describes a patient's cultural or racial background

Ethnography: A method of observational research that investigates culture in naturalistic settings using both qualitative and quantitative approaches

Etiology axis: The cause of a disease or injury

European Committee for Standardization (CEN): The European Committee for Standardization, consisting of the national standards bodies in Europe as well as associates representing broad industrial sectors and social and economic partners, adopts European Standards and other formal documents that promote free trade, the safety of workers and consumers, interoperability of networks, environmental protection, exploitation of research and development programs, and public procurement

Evaluation and management (E/M) codes: *Current Procedural Terminology* codes that describe patient encounters with healthcare professionals for assessment counseling and other routine healthcare services

Evaluation research: A design of research that examines the effectiveness of policies, programs, or organizations

Evidence-based clinical practice guideline: Explicit statement that guides clinical decision making and has been systematically developed from scientific evidence and clinical expertise to answer clinical questions

Evidence-based management: A management system in which practices based on research evidence will be effective and produce the outcomes they claim

Evidence-based medicine: Healthcare services based on clinical methods that have been thoroughly tested through controlled, peer-reviewed biomedical studies

Evidence-based practices: Services that use decision support systems and best practices in medicine rather than relying on subjective information

Evidence of insurability: A statement or proof of a person's physical condition and/or other factual information necessary to obtain healthcare insurance in certain situations

Exclusion: A specified condition or circumstance listed in an insurance policy for which the policy will not provide benefits; *See* **impairment rider**

Exclusive provider organization (EPO): Hybrid managed care organization that provides benefits to subscribers only when healthcare services are performed by network providers; sponsored by self-insured (self-funded) employers or associations and exhibits characteristics of both health maintenance organizations and preferred provider organizations

Executive dashboard: An information management system providing decision makers with regularly updated information on an organization's key strategic measures

Executive decision support system: *See* **executive information system**

Executive information system (EIS): An information system designed to combine financial and clinical information for use in the management of business affairs of a healthcare organization; *See* **executive decision support system**

Executive manager: A senior manager who oversees a broad functional area or group of departments or services, sets the organization's future direction, and monitors the organization's operations

Exempt employees: Specific groups of employees who are identified as not being covered by some or all of the provisions of the Fair Labor Standards Act

Expectancy theory: A theory of motivation that assumes people will choose behaviors because they expect that those behaviors to lead to certain outcomes

Expenses: Amounts that are charged as costs by an organization to the current year's activities of operation

Experimental research: 1. A research design used to establish cause and effect   2. A controlled investigation in which subjects are assigned randomly to groups that experience carefully controlled interventions that are manipulated by the experimenter according to a strict protocol; *See* **experimental study**

Experimental study: *See* **experimental research**

Expert decision support system: A decision support system that uses a set of rules or encoded concepts to construct a reasoning process

Expert system: A type of information system that supports the work of professionals engaged in the development or evaluation of complex activities that require high-level knowledge in a well-defined and usually limited area

Explanation of benefits (EOB): A statement issued to the insured and the healthcare provider by an insurer to explain the services provided, amounts billed, and payments made by a health plan

Explicit knowledge: Documents, databases, and other types of recorded and documented information

Exploding charges: Charges for items that must be reported separately but are used together, such as interventional radiology imaging and injection procedures

Expressed consent: The spoken or written permission granted by a patient to a healthcare provider that allows the provider to perform medical or surgical services

Extended care facility: A healthcare facility licensed by applicable state or local law to offer room and board, skilled nursing by a full-time registered nurse, intermediate care, or a combination of levels on a twenty-four-hour basis over a long period of time

Extensible markup language (XML): A standardized computer language that allows the interchange of data as structured text

External cause of injury code: *See* **E code**

External review: A performance or quality review conducted by a third-party payer or consultant hired for the purpose; *See* **audit**

External validity: An attribute of a study's design that allows its findings to be applied to other groups

Extraneous variable: *See* **confounding variable**

Extranet: A system of connections of private Internet networks outside an organization's firewall that uses Internet technology to enable collaborative applications among enterprises

Extreme immaturity: A condition referring to a newborn with a birth weight of fewer than 1000 grams and/or gestation of fewer than 28 completed weeks

Face sheet: Usually the first page of the health record that contains resident identification, demographics, original date of admission, insurance coverage or payment source, referral information, hospital stay dates, physician information, and discharge information, as well as the name of the responsible party, emergency and additional contacts, and the resident's diagnoses

Facilities, health: Buildings, including physical plant, equipment, and supplies, necessary in the provision of health services (for example, hospitals, nursing homes, and ambulatory care centers)

Facilities management: The functional oversight of a health-care organization's physical plant to ensure operational efficiency in an environment that is safe for patients, staff, and visitors

Facility-based registry: A registry that includes only cases from a particular type of healthcare facility, such as a hospital or clinic

Facility identification: A unique universal identification number across data systems

Facility-specific system: A computer information system developed exclusively to meet the needs of one healthcare organization

Facsimile: A machine that allows the remote transmission of text and graphics through telephone lines or a communication sent via this method; *See* **fax**

Factor comparison method: A complex quantitative method of job evaluation that combines elements of both the ranking and point methods

Fair Labor Standards Act of 1938 (FLSA): The federal legislation that sets the minimum wage and overtime payment regulations

Family and Medical Leave Act of 1993 (FMLA): The federal legislation that allows employees time off from work (up to twelve weeks) to care for themselves or their family members with the assurance of an equivalent position upon return to work

Family numbering: A filing system, sometimes used in clinic settings, in which an entire family is assigned one number

FASB: *See* **Financial Accounting Standards Board**

Favorable variance: The positive difference between the budgeted amount and the actual amount of a line item, that is, when actual revenue exceeds budget or actual expenses are less than budget

Fax: *See* **facsimile**

Faxing policy: A policy that outlines the steps to take for faxing individually identifiable health information and business records and usually limits what information may be faxed

FDA: *See* **Food and Drug Administration**

FECA: *See* **Federal Employees' Compensation Act**

Federal Employees' Compensation Act (FECA): The legislation enacted in 1916 to mandate workers' compensation for civilian federal employees, whose coverage includes lost wages, medical expenses, and survivors' benefits

Federal Food, Drug and Cosmetic Act (FFDCA): The Federal Food, Drug, and Cosmetic Act of 1938 (FFDCA): P.L. 75-717 (June 25, 1938) is the basic authority intended to ensure that foods are pure and wholesome, safe to eat, and produced under sanitary conditions; that drugs and devices are safe and effective for their intended uses; that cosmetics are safe and made from appropriate ingredients; and that all labeling and packaging is truthful, informative and not deceptive

Federal poverty level (FPL): The income qualification threshold established by the federal government for certain government entitlement programs

Federal Register: The daily publication of the U.S. Government Printing Office that reports all changes in regulations and federally mandated standards, including HCPCS and ICD-9-CM codes

Fee: Price assigned to a unit of medical or health service, such as a visit to a physician or a day in a hospital; may be unrelated to the actual cost of providing the service; *See* **charge**

Feeder system: An automated data system that feeds results into a comprehensive database

Feeder system: An information system that operates independently of a CPR system but provides data to it; *See* **source system**

Fee-for-service (FFS) reimbursement: A method of reimbursement through which providers retrospectively receive payment based on either billed charges for services provided or on annually updated fee schedules

Fee schedule: A list of healthcare services and procedures (usually CPT/HCPCS codes) and the charges associated with them developed by a third-party payer to represent the approved payment levels for a given insurance plan; *See* **table of allowances**

Felony: A serious crime such as murder, larceny, rape, or assault for which punishment is usually severe

FEP: *See* **Blue Cross and Blue Shield Federal Employee Program**

Fetal autopsy rate: The number of autopsies performed on intermediate and late fetal deaths for a given time period divided by the total number of intermediate and late fetal deaths for the same time period

Fetal death: The death of a product of human conception before its complete expulsion or extraction from the mother regardless of the duration of the pregnancy; *See* **stillbirth**

Fetal death rate: A proportion that compares the number of intermediate and/or late fetal deaths to the total number of live births and intermediate or late fetal deaths during the same period of time

FFDCA: *See* **Federal Food, Drug and Cosmetic Act**

FFS reimbursement: *See* **fee-for-service reimbursement** and **traditional fee-for-service reimbursement**

FI: *See* **fiscal intermediary**

File infector: A type of computer virus that attaches to program files, allowing it to be loaded when the program is loaded

File transfer protocol (FTP): A communications protocol that enables users to copy or move files between computer systems

FIM: *See* **functional independence measure**

Financial accounting: The mechanism that organizations use to fully comprehend and communicate their financial activities

Financial Accounting Standards Board (FASB): An independent organization that sets accounting standards for businesses in the private sector

Financial data: The data collected for the purpose of managing the assets of a business (for example, a healthcare organization, a product line); in healthcare, data derived from the charge generation documentation associated with the activities of care and then aggregated by specific customer grouping for financial analysis

Financial transaction: The exchange of goods or services for payment or the promise of payment

Firewall: A computer system or a combination of systems that provides a security barrier or supports an access control policy between two networks or between a network and the Internet

Fiscal intermediary (FI): An organization that contracts with the Centers for Medicare and Medicaid Services to serve as the financial agent between providers and the federal government in the local administration of Medicare Part B claims

Fiscal year: One business cycle or tax year, which may or may not coincide with the calendar year

Fishbone diagram: A performance improvement tool used to identify or classify the root causes of a problem or condition and to display the root causes graphically; *See* **cause-and-effect diagram**

Fixed assets: Long-term assets; *See* **capital assets** and **property, plant, and equipment**

Fixed budget: A type of budget based on expected capacity

Fixed cost: A cost that does not vary with the number of units of the item being purchased, in contrast to variable cost in which the cost varies per unit

Flat-panel display: The technology using liquid crystal display or other low-emission substances, once found primarily on laptops and now being used for desktop monitors, large-screen wall monitors, and high-density television

Flexible budget: A type of budget that is based on multiple levels of projected productivity (actual productivity triggers the levels to be used as the year progresses)

Flextime: A work schedule that gives employees some choice in the pattern of their work hours, usually around a core of midday hours

Flex years: A work arrangement in which employees can choose, at specific intervals, the number of hours they want to work each month over the next year

Float employee: An employee who is not assigned to a particular shift or function and who may fill in as needed in cases of standard employee absence or vacation

Flow chart: A graphic tool that uses standard symbols to visually display detailed information, including time and distance, of the sequential flow of work of an individual or a product as it progresses through a process

FLSA: *See* **Fair Labor Standards Act of 1938**

FMLA: *See* **Family and Medical Leave Act of 1993**

Focus: An organized form of charting narrative notes in which nursing terminology is used to explain the resident's health status and resulting nursing action

Focus charting: *See* **charting by exception**

Focused review: A process whereby a health record is analyzed to gather specific information about the diagnoses, treatments, or providers

Focused study: A study in which a researcher orally questions and conducts discussions with members of a group

FOIA: *See* **Freedom of Information Act**

Food and Drug Administration (FDA): The federal agency responsible for controlling the sale and use of pharmaceuticals, biological products, medical devices, food, cosmetics, and products that emit radiation, including the licensing of medications for human use; *See* **Federal Food Drug and Cosmetic Act**

Force-field analysis: A performance improvement tool used to identify specific drivers of, and barriers to, an organizational change so that positive factors can be reinforced and negative factors reduced

Forecast: To calculate or predict some future event or condition through study and analysis of available pertinent data

Forecast budget: A budgeting approach that simply divides the amount budgeted by the number of months in the fiscal period

Foreign key: A key attribute used to link one entity/table to another

Forms management policy: A policy that outlines the process for the creation of new forms

Formulary: A listing of drugs, classified by therapeutic category or disease class; in some health plans, providers are limited to prescribing only drugs listed on the plan's formulary

For profit: The tax status assigned to business entities that are owned by one or more individuals or organizations and that earn revenues in excess of expenditures that are subsequently paid out to the owners or stock holders

42 CFR Part 2: Federal confidentiality regulations governing and protecting records of clients receiving treatment for alcohol and drug abuse-related conditions

Foundation model: *See* **independent practice organization**

Fourteen principles of management: Henri Fayol's key points in the formulation of the administrative approach to management

FPL: *See* **federal poverty level**

Frame data: *See* **motion video**

Fraud: That which is done erroneously to purposely achieve gain from another

Fraud and abuse: The intentional and mistaken misrepresentation of reimbursement claims submitted to government-sponsored health programs

Freedom of Information Act (FOIA): The federal law, applicable only to federal agencies, through which individuals can seek access to information without the authorization of the person to whom the information applies

Freestanding facility: In Medicare terminology, an entity that furnishes healthcare services to beneficiaries and is not integrated with any other entity as a main provider, a department of a provider, or a provider-based entity

Free-text data: Data that are narrative in nature

Frequency distribution: A table or graph that displays the number of times (frequency) a particular observation occurs

Frequency distribution table: A table consisting of a set of classes or categories along with the numerical counts that correspond to nominal and ordinal data

Frequency polygon: A type of line graph that represents a frequency distribution

FTE: *See* **full-time equivalent**

FTP: *See* **file transfer protocol**

Full-time employee: An employee who works forty hours per week, eighty hours per two-week period, or eight hours per day

Full-time equivalent (FTE): A statistic representing the number of full-time employees as calculated by the reported number of hours worked by all employees, including part-time and temporary, during a specific time period

Fully Specified Name: In SNOMED CT, the unique text assigned to a concept that completely describes that concept

Functional independence measure (FIM): A measure that addresses a patient's functional status in six domains: self-care, sphincter control, mobility, locomotion, social cognition, and communication

Functional requirement: A statement that describes the processes a computer system should perform to derive the technical specifications, or desired behavior, of a system

Functional status: A commonly used measure of a patient's mental and/or physical abilities

Functional status domain: A classification made up of six activities of daily living, including upper and lower body dressing, bathing, toileting, transferring, and moving

Function axis: Physiological or chemical disorders and alterations resulting from a disease or injury

Fund balance: In a not-for-profit setting, the entity's net assets or resources remaining after subtracting liabilities that are owed; in a for-profit organization, the owner's equity

Future value: The total dollar amount of an investment at a later point in time, including any earned or implied interest

Fuzzy logic: An analytic technique used in data mining to handle imprecise concepts

GAAP: *See* **generally accepted accounting principles**

GAF: *See* **geographic adjustment factor**

Gantt chart: A graphic tool used to plot tasks in project management that shows the duration of project tasks and overlapping tasks

GASB: *See* **Government Accounting Standards Board**

Gatekeeper: The healthcare provider or entity responsible for determining the healthcare services a patient or client may access; for instance, a primary care physician, a utilization review or case management agency, or a managed care organization

Gender: The biological sex of the patient as recorded at the start of care

General consent: *See* **general consent to treatment**

General consent to treatment: A consent signed upon admission to the facility that allows the clinical staff to provide care and treatment for the resident and that usually includes the resident's agreement to pay for the services provided by the facility, to assign insurance benefits to the facility, and to allow the facility to obtain or release health records for payment purposes; *See* **general consent**

General health record documentation policy: A policy that outlines documentation practices within the facility

Generalizability: The ability to apply research results, data, or observations to groups not originally under study

General ledger: A master list of individual revenue and expense accounts maintained by an organization

General ledger (G/L) key: The two- or three-digit number in the chargemaster that assigns each item to a particular section of the general ledger in a healthcare facility's accounting section

Generally accepted accounting principles (GAAP): An accepted set of accounting principles, or standards, and recognized procedures central to financial accounting and reporting

Generic screening: *See* **occurrence screening**

Genetic algorithms: Optimization techniques that can be used to improve other data-mining algorithms so that they derive the best model for a given set of data

Geographic adjustment factor (GAF): Adjustment to the national standardized Medicare fee schedule relative value components used to account for differences in the cost of practicing medicine in different geographic areas of the country

Geographic information system (GIS): A decision support system that is capable of assembling, storing, manipulating, and displaying geographically referenced data and information

Geographic practice cost index (GPCI): An index developed by the Centers for Medicare and Medicaid Services to measure the differences in resource costs among fee schedule areas compared to the national average in the three components of the relative value unit: physician work, practice expenses, and malpractice coverage

Geometric mean length of stay (GMLOS): An adjusted length of stay for all-patient allowances for outliers, transfers, and negative outliers that would otherwise skew the data

Gesture recognition technology: *See* **intelligent character recognition technology**

GIS: *See* **geographic information system**

G/L key: *See* **general ledger key**

Global Medical Device Nomenclature: A collection of internationally recognized terms used to accurately describe and catalogue medical devices, in particular, the products used in the diagnosis, prevention, monitoring, treatment or alleviation of disease or injury in humans

Global payment: A form of reimbursement used for radiological and other procedures that combines the professional and technical components of the procedures and disperses payments as lump sums to be distributed between the physician and the healthcare facility

Global payment method: Method of payment in which the third party payer makes one consolidated payment to cover the services of multiple providers who are treating a single episode of care

Global surgery package: A CPT code denoting a normal surgical procedure with no complications that includes all of the elements needed to perform the procedure

Global surgery payment: A payment made for surgical procedures that includes the provision of all healthcare services, from the treatment decision through postoperative patient care

GMLOS: *See* **geometric mean length of stay**

Goal: A specific description of the services or deliverable goods to be provided as the result of a business process

Going concern: An organization that can be assumed to continue indefinitely unless otherwise stated

Government Accounting Standards Board (GASB): The federal agency that sets the accounting standards to be followed by government entities

GPCI: *See* **geographic practice cost index**

GPWW: *See* **group practice without walls**

Grace period: An amount of time beyond a due date during which a payment may be made without incurring penalties; in healthcare, the specific time (usually thirty-one days) following the premium due date during which insurance remains in effect and a policyholder may pay the premium without penalty or loss of benefits

Granularity: The relative level of detail or the smallest amount of discrete information that can be directly retrieved (higher granularity yields greater detail)

Graph: A graphic tool used to show numerical data in a pictorial representation

Graphical user interface (GUI): A style of computer interface in which typed commands are replaced by images that represent tasks, for example, small pictures (icons) that represent the tasks, functions, and programs performed by a software program

Graphics-based decision support system: A decision support system in which the knowledge base consists primarily of graphical data and the user interface exploits the use of graphical display

Great person theory: The belief that some people have natural (innate) leadership skills

Grievance: A formal, written description of a complaint or disagreement

Grievance procedures: The steps employees may follow to seek resolution of disagreements with management on job-related issues

Gross autopsy rate: The number of inpatient autopsies conducted during a given time period divided by the total number of inpatient deaths for the same time period

Gross death rate: The number of inpatient deaths that occurred during a given time period divided by the total number of inpatient discharges, including deaths, for the same time period

Grouper: A computer software program that automatically assigns prospective payment groups on the basis of clinical codes

Group health insurance: A prepaid medical plan that covers the healthcare expenses of an organization's full-time employees

Grouping: A system for assigning patients to a classification scheme via a computer software program

Group practice: An organization of physicians who share office space and administrative support services to achieve economies of scale, often a clinic or ambulatory care center

Group practice model: A closed panel health maintenance organization (HMO) in which the HMO contracts with a medical group and reimburses the group on a fee-for-service or capitation basis; *See* **closed panel** and **network model**

Group practice without walls (GPWW): A type of managed care contract that allows physicians to maintain their own offices and share administrative services; *See* **clinic without walls**, or **CWW**

Group process: An intragroup activity of relevance to organizational effectiveness that includes elements such as socialization of new members and conflict resolution

Groupthink: An implicit form of group consensus in which openness and effective decision making are sacrificed to conformity

Groupware: An Internet technology that consolidates documents from different information systems within an organization into a tightly integrated workflow

Guarantor: Person who is responsible for paying the bill or guarantees payment for healthcare services; adult patients are often their own guarantors, but parents guarantee payments for the healthcare costs of their children

GUI: *See* **graphical user interface**

HAART: *See* **highly active antiretroviral therapy**

Habit: An activity repeated so often that it becomes automatic

Hacker: An individual who bypasses a computer system's access control by taking advantage of system security weaknesses and/or by appropriating the password of an authorized user

Halo effect: A bias that occurs when someone allows certain information to influence a decision disproportionately

Hard code: A code applied through a healthcare organization's chargemaster

Hard-coded: An information system term referring to the fact that a screen displays certain content in accordance with software instructions that cannot be manipulated by the user for purposes of changing the content

Hard coding: The process of attaching a CPT/HCPCS code to a procedure located on the facility's chargemaster so that the code will automatically be included on the patient's bill

Harvard relative value scale study: Research conducted at Harvard University by William Hsiao and Peter Braun on establishing the appropriate relative values for physician services

HAVEN: *See* **Home Assessment Validation and Entry**

Hawthorne effect: A research study that found that novelty, attention, and interpersonal relations have a motivating effect on performance

Hay Guide Chart/Profile Method of Job Evaluation: *See* **Hay method**

Hay method: A modification of the point method of job evaluation that numerically measures the levels of three major compensable factors: know-how, problem-solving ability, and accountability; *See* **Hay Guide Chart/Profile Method of Job Evaluation**

HCFA: *See* **Health Care Financing Administration**

HCFA Common Procedural Coding System (HCPCS): Previous name for the Healthcare Common Procedural Coding System

HCFA-1500: Previous name for **CMS-1500**

HCPCS: *See* **Healthcare Common Procedural Coding System** and **HCFA Common Procedural Coding System**

HCQIP: *See* **Health Care Quality Improvement Program**

HCRIS: *See* **healthcare provider cost report information system**

HCUP: *See* **Healthcare Cost and Utilization Project**

Health: A state of complete physical, mental, and social well-being and not merely the absence of disease or infirmity

Healthcare claims and payment/advice transaction: An electronic transmission sent by a health plan to a provider's financial representative for the purpose of providing information about payments and/or payment processing and information about the transfer of funds

Healthcare clearinghouse: A public or private entity such as a billing service, repricing company, community health management information system, or community health information system or a value-added network that either processes or facilitates the processing of health information received from another entity in a nonstandard format or containing nonstandard data content into standard data elements or standard transactions or receives a standard transaction from another entity and processes or facilitates the processing of health information into nonstandard format or nonstandard data content for the receiving entity

Healthcare Common Procedural Coding System (HCPCS): A classification system that identifies healthcare procedures, equipment, and supplies for claim submission purposes; the three levels are as follows: I, *Current Procedural Terminology* codes, developed by the AMA; II, codes for equipment, supplies, and services not covered by *Current Procedural Terminology* codes as well as modifiers that can be used with all levels of codes, developed by CMS; and III (eliminated December 31, 2003 to comply with HIPAA), local codes developed by regional Medicare Part B carriers and used to report physicians' services and supplies to Medicare for reimbursement

Healthcare Cost and Utilization Project (HCUP): A group of healthcare databases and related software tools developed through collaboration by the federal government, state governments, and industry to create a national information resource for patient-level healthcare data

Healthcare Facilities Accreditation Program (HFAP): An accreditation program managed by the American

Osteopathic Association that offers services to a number of healthcare facilities and services, including laboratories, ambulatory care clinics, ambulatory surgery centers, behavioral health and substance abuse treatment facilities, physical rehabilitation facilities, acute care hospitals, critical access hospitals, and hospitals providing postdoctoral training for osteopathic physicians

Health Care Financing Administration (HCFA): Previous name of the Centers for Medicare and Medicaid Services

Healthcare informatics: The field of information science concerned with the management of all aspects of health data and information through the application of computers and computer technologies; *See* **clinical informatics, informatics, nursing informatics**

Healthcare Information and Management Systems Society (HIMSS): A national membership association that provides leadership in healthcare for the management of technology, information, and change

Healthcare information system (HIS): A transactional system used in healthcare organizations (for example, patient admitting, accounting, and receivables); *See* **hospital information system**

Healthcare Information Systems Steering Committee: An interdisciplinary team of healthcare professionals generally responsible for developing a strategic information system plan, prioritizing information system projects, and coordinating IS-related projects across the enterprise

Healthcare Integrity and Protection Data Bank (HIPDB): A national database that collects information on cases of healthcare fraud and abuse

Healthcare operations: Certain activities undertaken by or on behalf of, a covered entity, including those involved with quality assessment, performance improvement, peer review, clinical training, underwriting, legal services, compliance, and business management functions

Healthcare practitioner: A clinical professional who is directly responsible for providing patient services

Healthcare practitioner identification: A unique national identification number assigned to the healthcare practitioner of record for each encounter

Healthcare provider: A provider of diagnostic, medical, and surgical care as well as the services or supplies related to the health of an individual and any other person or organization that issues reimbursement claims or is paid for healthcare in the normal course of business

Healthcare provider cost report information system (HCRIS): A system of Medicare cost report files containing information on provider characteristics, utilization data, and cost and charge data by cost center

Health Care Quality Improvement Program (HCQIP): A quality initiative begun in 1992 by the Health Care Financing Administration and implemented by peer review organizations that uses patterns of care analysis and collaboration with practitioners, beneficiaries, providers, plans, and other purchasers of healthcare services to develop scientifically based quality indicators and to identify and implement opportunities for healthcare improvement

Healthcare services: Processes that directly or indirectly contribute to the health and well-being of patients, such as medical, nursing, and other health-related services

Health delivery network: *See* **integrated provider organization**

Health Industry Business Communications Council (HIBCC): A subgroup of the American Standards Committee X12 that focuses on electronic data interchange for billing transactions

Health informatics standards: A set of standards that describe accepted methods for collecting, maintaining, and/or transferring healthcare data among computer systems

Health information: According to the HIPAA privacy rule, any information (verbal or written) created or received by a healthcare provider, health plan, public health authority, employer, life insurer, school or university, or healthcare clearinghouse that relates to the physical or mental health of an individual, provision of healthcare to an individual, or payment for provision of healthcare

Health information management (HIM): An allied health profession that is responsible for ensuring the availability, accuracy, and protection of the clinical information that is needed to deliver healthcare services and to make appropriate healthcare-related decisions

Health information management (HIM) professional: An individual who has received professional training at the associate or baccalaureate degree level in the management of health data and information flow throughout healthcare delivery systems; formerly known as **medical record technician** or **medical record administrator**

Health information services department: The department in a healthcare organization that is responsible for maintaining patient care records in accordance with external and internal rules and regulations; *See* **medical records department**

Health Information Standards Board (HISB): A subgroup of the American National Standards Institute that acts as an umbrella organization for groups interested in developing healthcare computer messaging standards

Health Insurance Portability and Accountability Act of 1996 (HIPAA): The federal legislation enacted to provide continuity of health coverage, control fraud and abuse in healthcare, reduce healthcare costs, and guarantee the security and privacy of health information. The act limits exclusion for preexisting medical conditions, prohibits discrimination against employees and dependents based on health status, guarantees availability of health insurance to small employers, and guarantees renewability of insurance to all employees regardless of size

Health insurance prospective payment system (HIPPS) code: A five-character code used for Medicare billing by skilled nursing facilities

Health insurance query for home health agencies (HIQH): An online transaction system that provides information on home health and hospice episodes for specific Medicare beneficiaries

Health Integrity and Protection Data Bank: A database maintained by the federal government to provide information on fraud-and-abuse findings against U.S. healthcare providers

Health Level Seven (HL7): A standards development organization accredited by the American National Standards Institute that addresses issues at the seventh, or application, level of healthcare systems interconnections

Health maintenance organization (HMO): Entity that combines the provision of healthcare insurance and the delivery of healthcare services, characterized by: (1) organized healthcare delivery system to a geographic area, (2) set of basic and supplemental health maintenance and treatment services, (3) voluntarily enrolled members, and (4) predetermined fixed, periodic prepayments for members' coverage

Health Maintenance Organization (HMO) Act: The 1973 federal legislation that outlined the requirements for federal qualifications of health maintenance organizations, consisting of legal and organizational structures, financial strength requirements, marketing provisions, and healthcare delivery

Health maintenance organization (HMO) referral: *See* **source of admission**

Health management information system (HMIS): An information system whose purpose is to provide reports on routine operations and processing (for example, a pharmacy inventory system, radiological system, or patient-tracking system)

Health plan: An entity that provides or pays the cost of medical care on behalf of enrolled individuals; includes group health plans, health insurance issuers, health maintenance organizations, and other welfare benefit plans such as Medicare, Medicaid, CHAMPUS, and Indian Health Services

Health Plan Employer Information Data Set (HEDIS): A set of performance measures developed by the National Commission for Quality Assurance that are designed to provide purchasers and consumers of healthcare with the information they need to compare the performance of managed care plans

Health record: A paper- or computer-based tool for collecting and storing information about the healthcare services provided to a patient in a single healthcare facility; also called a patient record, medical record, resident record, or client record, depending on the healthcare setting

Health record analysis: A concurrent or ongoing review of health record content performed by caregivers or HIM professionals while the patient is still receiving inpatient services to ensure the quality of the services being provided and the completeness of the documentation being maintained

Health record committee policy: A policy that outlines the goals of the committee, the audit tools used, the number of audits required and specific time frames for their completion, and the results-reporting mechanisms

Health record department access policy: A policy that outlines how physicians are notified of records needing signatures

Health record number: A unique numeric or alphanumeric identifier assigned to each patient's record upon admission to a healthcare facility

Health record ownership: The generally accepted principle that individual health records are maintained and owned by the healthcare organization that creates them but that patients have certain rights of control over the release of patient-identifiable (confidential) information

Health record security program: A set of processes and procedures designed to protect the data and information stored in a health record system from damage and unauthorized access

Health Resources and Services Administration (HRSA): The national organization that administers the State Children's Health Insurance Program along with the Centers for Medicare and Medicaid Services

Health science librarian: A professional librarian who manages a medical library

Health services research: Research conducted on the subject of healthcare delivery that examines organizational structures and systems as well as the effectiveness and efficiency of healthcare services

HEDIS: *See* **Health Plan Employer Data and Information Set**

Help desk: A central access point to information system support services that attempts to resolve users' technical problems, sometimes with the use of decision-making algorithms, and tracks problems until their resolution

Heterogeneity: The state or fact of containing various components

HFAP: *See* **Healthcare Facilities Accreditation Program**

HH: *See* **home health**

HHA: *See* **home health agency**

HH PPS: *See* **home health prospective payment system**

HHRG: *See* **home health resource group**

HIBCC: *See* **Health Industry Business Communications Council**

Hierarchical system: A system structured with broad groupings that can be further subdivided into more narrowly defined group or detailed entities

Hierarchy: An authoritarian organizational structure in which each member is assigned a specific rank that reflects his or her level of decision-making authority within the organization

Hierarchy of needs: Maslow's theory that suggested that human needs are organized hierarchically from basic physiological requirements to creative motivations

Highly active antiretroviral therapy (HAART): A type of therapy that consists of multiple drugs commonly given to HIV-positive individuals before they develop AIDS

Hill-Burton Act: The federal legislation enacted in 1946 as the Hospital Survey and Construction Act to authorize grants for states to construct new hospitals and, later, to modernize old ones

HIM: *See* **health information management**

HIM professional: *See* **health information management professional**

HIMSS: *See* **Healthcare Information and Management Systems Society**

HIPAA: *See* **Health Insurance Portability and Accountability Act of 1996**

HIPAA privacy rule: *See* **Health Insurance Portability and Accountability Act of 1996** and **privacy rule**

HIPAA security rule: *See* **Health Insurance Portability and Accountability Act of 1996** and **security rule**

HIPDB: *See* **Healthcare Integrity and Protection Data Bank**

Hippocratic oath: An oath created by ancient Greeks to embody a code of medical ethics

HIPPS code: *See* **health insurance prospective payment system code**

HIQH: *See* **health insurance query for home health agencies**

HIS: *See* **healthcare information system**

HIS: *See* **hospital information system**

HISB: *See* **Health Information Standards Board**

Histocompatibility: The immunologic similarity between an organ donor and a transplant recipient

Histogram: A graphic technique used to display the frequency distribution of continuous data (interval or ratio data) as either numbers or percentages in a series of bars

Historical cost: The original cost of an asset; considered the more objective measurement for financial reporting purposes

Historical research: A research design used to investigate past events

History: The pertinent information about a patient, including chief complaint, past and present illnesses, family history, social history, and review of body systems

History and physical (H&P): The pertinent information about the patient, including chief complaint, past and present illnesses, family history, social history, and review of body systems

History and physical documentation requirements policy: A policy that specifies the detail required in the history and physical examination done by the physician or physician extender

HIV: *See* **human immunodeficiency virus**

HL7: *See* **Health Level Seven**

HME: *See* **home medical equipment**

HMIS: *See* **health management information system**

HMO: *See* **health maintenance organization**

HMO Act: *See* **Health Maintenance Organization Act**

HMO referral: *See* **health maintenance organization referral**

HOLAP: *See* **hybrid online analytical processing**

Hold harmless: A term used to refer to the financial protections that ensure that cancer hospitals recoup all losses due to the differences in their ambulatory payment classification payments and the pre-APC payments for Medicare outpatient services

Home Assessment Validation and Entry (HAVEN): A type of data-entry software used to collect Outcome and Assessment Information Set (OASIS) data and then transmit them to state databases; imports and exports data in standard OASIS record format, maintains agency/patient/employee information, enforces data integrity through rigorous edit checks, and provides comprehensive online help

Home care: *See* **home health**

Home health (HH): An umbrella term that refers to the medical and nonmedical services provided to patients and their families in their places of residence; *See* **home care**

Home health agency (HHA): A program or organization that provides a blend of home-based medical and social services to homebound patients and their families for the purpose of promoting, maintaining, or restoring health or of minimizing the effects of illness, injury, or disability

Home healthcare: The medical and/or personal care provided to individuals and families in their place of residence with the goal of promoting, maintaining, or restoring health or minimizing the effects of disabilities and illnesses, including terminal illnesses

Home health prospective payment system (HH PPS): The reimbursement system developed by the Centers for Medicare and Medicaid Services to cover home health services provided to Medicare beneficiaries

Home health resource group (HHRG): A classification system with eighty home health episode rates established to support the prospective reimbursement of covered home care and rehabilitation services provided to Medicare beneficiaries during sixty-day episodes of care

Home medical equipment: *See* **durable medical equipment**

Horizontally integrated system: *See* **integrated provider organization**

Hospice: An interdisciplinary program of palliative care and supportive services that addresses the physical, spiritual, social, and economic needs of terminally ill patients and their families

Hospice care: The medical care provided to persons with life expectancies of six months or less who elect to forgo standard treatment of their illness and to receive only palliative care

Hospital: A healthcare entity that has an organized medical staff and permanent facilities that include inpatient beds and continuous medical/nursing services and that provides diagnostic and therapeutic services for patients as well as overnight accommodations and nutritional services

Hospital-acquired infection: *See* **nosocomial infection**

Hospital-affiliated ambulatory surgery center: An ambulatory surgery center that is owned and operated by a hospital but is a separate entity with respect to its licensure, accreditation, governance, professional supervision, administrative functions, clinical services, record keeping, and financial and accounting systems

Hospital ambulatory care: All hospital-directed preventive, therapeutic, and rehabilitative services provided by physicians and their surrogates to patients who are not hospital inpatients

Hospital autopsy: A postmortem (after death) examination performed on the body of a person who has at some time been a hospital patient by a hospital pathologist or a physician of the medical staff who has been delegated the responsibility; *See* **hospital inpatient autopsy**

Hospital autopsy rate: The total number of autopsies performed by a hospital pathologist for a given time period divided by the number of deaths of hospital patients (inpatients and outpatients) whose bodies were available for autopsy for the same time period

Hospital autopsy rate, adjusted: The proportion of death of hospital patients following which the bodies were available for autopsy and hospital autopsies were performed; *See* **available for hospital autopsy**

Hospital-based ambulatory care center: An organized hospital facility that provides nonemergency medical or dental services to patients who are not assigned to a bed as inpatients during the time services are rendered (an emergency department in which services are provided to nonemergency patients is not considered an ambulatory care center)

Hospital-based ambulatory surgery center: A department of an inpatient facility that provides same-day surgical services using the facility's equipment, staff, and support services

Hospital-based outpatient care: A subset of ambulatory care that utilizes a hospital's staff, equipment, and resources to render preventive and/or corrective healthcare services

Hospital death rate: The number of inpatient deaths for a given period of time divided by the total number of live discharges and deaths for the same time period

Hospital discharge abstract system: A group of databases compiled from aggregate data on all patients discharged from a hospital

Hospital identification: A unique institutional number within a data collection system

Hospital information system (HIS): The comprehensive database containing all the clinical, administrative, financial, and demographic information about each patient served by a hospital

Hospital inpatient: A patient who is provided with room, board, and continuous general nursing services in an area of an acute care facility where patients generally stay at least overnight

Hospital inpatient autopsy: A postmortem (after death) examination performed on the body of a patient who died during an inpatient hospitalization by a hospital pathologist or a physician of the medical staff who has been delegated the responsibility

Hospital inpatient beds: Accommodations with supporting services (such as food, laundry, and housekeeping) for hospital inpatients, excluding those for the newborn nursery but including incubators and bassinets in nurseries for premature or sick newborn infants

Hospitalist: Physicians employed by teaching hospitals to play the role that admitting physicians fulfill in hospitals that are not affiliated with medical training programs

Hospitalization: See **inpatient hospitalization**

Hospitalization insurance (Medicare Part A): A federal program that covers the costs associated with inpatient hospitalization as well as other healthcare services provided to Medicare beneficiaries

Hospital live birth: In an inpatient facility, the complete expulsion or extraction of a product of human conception from the mother, regardless of the duration of pregnancy, which, after such expulsion or extraction, breathes or shows any other evidence of life, such as beating of the heart, pulsation of the umbilical cord, or definite movement of voluntary muscles

Hospital newborn bassinet: Accommodations including incubators and isolettes in the newborn nursery with supporting services (such as food, laundry, and housekeeping) for hospital newborn inpatients

Hospital newborn inpatient: A patient born in the hospital at the beginning of the current inpatient hospitalization

Hospital outpatient: A hospital patient who receives services in one or more of a hospital's facilities when he or she is not currently an inpatient or a home care patient

Hospital outpatient care unit: An organized unit of a hospital that provides facilities and medical services exclusively or primarily to patients who are generally ambulatory and who do not currently require or are not currently receiving services as an inpatient of the hospital

Hospital Standardization Program: An early twentieth-century survey mechanism instituted by the American College of Surgeons and aimed at identifying quality-of-care problems and improving patient care; precursor to the survey program offered by the Joint Commission on Accreditation of Healthcare Organizations

Hot site: A duplicate of the organization's critical systems stored in a remote location

H&P: *See* **history and physical**

HRSA: *See* **Health Resources and Services Administration**

HTML: *See* **hypertext markup language**

HTTP: *See* **hypertext transport protocol**

Human–computer interface: The device used by humans to access and enter data into a computer system, such as a keyboard on a PC, personal digital assistant, voice recognition system, and so on

Human immunodeficiency virus (HIV): The virus that causes acquired immunodeficiency syndrome (AIDS)

Human relations movement: A management philosophy emphasizing the shift from a mechanistic view of workers to concern for their satisfaction at work

Human subjects: Individuals whose physiologic or behavioral characteristics and responses are the object of study in a research program

Hybrid online analytical processing (HOLAP): A data access methodology that is coupled tightly with the architecture of the database management system to allow the user to perform business analyses

Hybrid record: A health record that is includes both paper and electronic elements

Hypertext markup language (HTML): A standardized computer language that allows the electronic transfer of information and communications among many different information systems

Hypertext transport protocol (HTTP): A communications protocol that enables the use of hypertext linking

Hypothesis: A statement that describes a research question in measurable terms

I

ICD-9-CM: *See* **International Classification of Diseases, Ninth Revision, Clinical Modification**

ICD-O-2: *See* **International Classification of Diseases for Oncology, Second Edition**

ICD-10: *See* **International Classification of Diseases, Tenth Revision**

ICR technology: *See* **intelligent character recognition technology**

Identifier standards: Recommended methods for assigning unique identifiers to individuals (patients and clinical providers), corporate providers, and healthcare vendors and suppliers

Identity management: In the master patient index, policies and procedures that manage patient identity, such as prohibiting the same record number for duplicate patients or duplicate records for one patient

IDR technology: *See* **intelligent document recognition technology**

IDS: *See* **integrated delivery system**

IEEE: *See* **Institute of Electrical and Electronics Engineers**

IETF: *See* **Internet Engineering Task Force**

IFA: *See* **indirect immunofluorescence assay**

IHS: *See* **Indian Health Service**

Image processing: The ability of a computer to create a graphic representation of a text block, photograph, drawing, or other image and make it available throughout an information system

Imaging technology: Computer software designed to combine health record text files with diagnostic imaging files

Impact analysis: A collective term used to refer to any study that determines the benefit of a proposed project, including cost-benefit analysis, return on investment, benefits realization study, or qualitative benefit study

Impairment rider: *See* **exclusion**

Implementation phase: The third phase of the systems development life cycle during which a comprehensive plan is developed and instituted to ensure that the new information system is effectively implemented within the organization

Implied consent: The type of permission that is inferred when a patient voluntarily submits to treatment

Incentive: Something that stimulates or encourages an individual to work harder

Incentive pay: A system of bonuses and rewards based on employee productivity; often used in transcription areas of healthcare facilities

Incidence: The number of new cases of a specific disease

Incidence rate: A computation that compares the number of new cases of a specific disease for a given time period to the population at risk for the disease during the same time period

Incident: An occurrence in a medical facility that is inconsistent with accepted standards of care

Incident report: A quality/performance management tool used to collect data and information about potentially compensable events (events that may result in death or serious injury)

Incident report review: An analysis of incident reports or an evaluation of descriptions of adverse events

Income statement: A statement that summarizes an organization's revenue and expense accounts using totals accumulated during the fiscal year

Incomplete records policy: A policy that outlines how physicians are notified of records needing signatures

Incremental budgeting: A budgeting approach in which the financial database of the past is increased by a given percentage and adjustments are made for anticipated changes, with an added inflation factor

Indemnification statement: A statement that exempts the signer from incurring liabilities or penalties

Indemnity health insurance: Traditional, fee-for-service healthcare plan in which the policyholder pays a monthly premium and a percentage of the usual, customary, and reasonable healthcare costs and the patient can select the provider

Indemnity plan: Health insurance coverage provided in the form of cash payments to patients or providers; *See* **indemnity health insurance**

Independent consultant: An individual who works as a contractor to provide coding services to healthcare facilities

Independent practice organization (IPO) or association (IPA): An open-panel health maintenance organization that provides contract healthcare services to subscribers through independent physicians who treat patients in their own offices; the HMO reimburses the IPA on a capitated basis; the IPA may reimburse the physicians on a fee-for-service or a capitated basis; *See* **individual practice association model** and **foundation model**

Independent variable: An antecedent factor that researchers manipulate directly

Index: An organized (usually alphabetical) list of specific data that serves to guide, indicate, or otherwise facilitate reference to the data

Indian Health Service (IHS): The federal agency within the Department of Health and Human Services that is responsible for providing federal healthcare services to American Indians and Alaska natives

Indicator: 1. An activity, event, occurrence, or outcome that is to be monitored and evaluated under a Joint Commission on Accreditation of Healthcare Organizations standard in order to determine whether those aspects conform to standards; commonly relates to the structure, process, and/or outcome of an important aspect of care   2. A measure used to determine an organization's performance over time

Indicator measurement system: An indicator-based monitoring system developed by the Joint Commission on Accreditation of Healthcare Organizations for accredited organizations and meant to provide hospitals with information on their performance

Indirect costs: Costs that cannot be traced to a given cost object without resorting to some arbitrary method of assignment

Indirect immunofluorescence assay (IFA): One of the diagnostic tests used to confirm infection with the human immunodeficiency virus (HIV)

Indirect obstetric death: The death of a woman that resulted from a previously existing disease (or a disease that developed during pregnancy, labor, or the puerperium) that was not due to obstetric causes, although the physiologic effects of pregnancy were partially responsible for the death

Individual: According to the HIPAA privacy rule, a person who is the subject of protected health information

Individually identifiable data: Personal information that can be linked to a specific patient, such as age, gender, date of birth, and address

Individually identifiable health information: According to HIPAA privacy provisions, the information that specifically identifies the patient to whom the information relates

Individual practice association model: *See* **independent practice organization**

Individual provider: A health professional who delivers or is professionally responsible for delivering services to a patient, is exercising independent judgment in the care of the patient, and is not under the immediate supervision of another healthcare professional

Induced termination of pregnancy: The purposeful interruption of an intrauterine pregnancy that was not intended to produce a live-born infant and that did not result in a live birth

Inductive reasoning: A process of creating conclusions based on a limited number of observations

Infant death: The death of a liveborn infant at any time from the moment of birth to the end of the first year of life (364 days, 23 hours, 59 minutes from the moment of birth)

Infant mortality rate: The number of deaths of individuals under one year of age during a given time period divided by the number of live births reported for the same time period

Infection control: A system for the prevention of communicable diseases that concentrates on protecting healthcare workers and patients against exposure to disease-causing organisms and promotes compliance with applicable legal requirements through early identification of potential sources of contamination and implementation of policies and procedures that limit the spread of disease

Inference engine: Specialized computer software that tries to match conditions in rules to data elements in a repository (when a match is found, the engine executes the rule, which results in the occurrence of a specified action)

Inferential statistics: A set of statistical techniques that allows researchers to make generalizations about a population's characteristics (parameters) on the basis of a sample's characteristics

Informatics: A field of study that focuses on the use of technology to improve access to, and utilization of, information

Information: Factual data that have been collected, combined, analyzed, interpreted, and/or converted into a form that can be used for a specific purpose

Information asset: Information that has value for an organization

Information cycle: The cycle of gathering, recording, processing, storing, sharing, transmitting, retrieving, and deleting information

Information kiosk: A computer station located within a healthcare facility that patients and families can use to access information

Information management: The acquisition, organization, analysis, storage, retrieval, and dissemination of information to support decision-making activities

Information modeling: The use of clinical code sets with application software to create information that is meaningful to the end user

Information resource management: A concept that assumes that information is a valuable resource that must be managed, regardless of the form it takes or the medium in which it is stored

Information science: The study of the nature and principles of information

Information security program: A program that includes all activities of an organization related to information security, including policies, standards, training, technical and procedural controls, risk assessment, auditing and monitoring, and assigned responsibility for management of the program

Information system (IS): An automated system that uses computer hardware and software to record, manipulate, store, recover, and disseminate data (that is, a system that receives and processes input and provides output); often used interchangeably with **information technology (IT)**

Information systems (IS) department: The department in a healthcare organization that is responsible for ensuring that the organization has the technical infrastructure and staff required to operate and manage its computer-based systems

Information technology (IT): Computer technology (hardware and software) combined with telecommunications technology (data, image, and voice networks); often used interchangeably with **information system (IS)**

Information technology (IT) professional: An individual who works with computer technology in the process of managing health information

Information technology (IT) strategy: An organization's information technology goals, objectives, and strategic plans, which serve as a guide to the procurement of information systems within an organization

Informed consent: 1. A legal term referring to a patient's right to make his or her own treatment decisions based on the knowledge of the treatment to be administered or the procedure to be performed   2. An individual's voluntary agreement to participate in research or to undergo a diagnostic, therapeutic, or preventive medical procedure

Infrastructure: The underlying framework and features of an information system

Initiating structure: A leadership orientation toward tasks, procedures, goals, and production

Injury severity score (ISS): An overall severity measurement maintained in the trauma registry and calculated from the abbreviated injury scores for the three most severe injuries of each patient

Innovator: An early adopter of change who are eager to experiment with new ways of doing things

Inpatient: A patient who is provided with room, board, and continuous general nursing services in an area of an acute care facility where patients generally stay at least overnight; *See* **hospital inpatient**

Inpatient admission: An acute care facility's formal acceptance of a patient who is to be provided with room, board, and continuous nursing service in an area of the facility where patients generally stay at least overnight

Inpatient bed occupancy rate: The total number of inpatient service days for a given time period divided by the total number of inpatient bed count days for the same time period; *See* **percentage of occupancy**

Inpatient coding compliance: The accurate and complete assignment of ICD-9-CM diagnostic and procedural codes, along with appropriate sequencing (for example, identification of principal diagnosis) to determine the appropriate diagnosis-related group and resultant payment

Inpatient days of stay: *See* **length of stay**

Inpatient discharge: The termination of hospitalization through the formal release of an inpatient from a hospital

Inpatient hospitalization: The period during an individual's life when he or she is a patient in a single hospital without interruption except by possible intervening leaves of absence

Inpatient long term care hospital (LTCH): A healthcare facility that has an average length of stay greater than 25 days, with patients classified into distinct diagnosis groups called LCS-DRGs; prospective payment system for LTCHs was established by CMS and went into effect beginning in 2002

Inpatient psychiatric facility (IPF): A healthcare facility that offers psychiatric medical care on an inpatient basis; CMS established a prospective payment system for reimbursing these types of facilities using the current DRGs for inpatient hospitals

Inpatient psychiatric facility PPS (IPFPPS): A per diem prospective payment system that is based on fifteen diagnosis-related groups which became effective on January 1, 2005

Inpatient rehabilitation facility (IRF): A healthcare facility that specializes in providing services to patients who have suffered a disabling illness or injury in an effort to help them achieve or maintain their optimal level of functioning, self-care, and independence

Inpatient rehabilitation facility PPS (IRFPPS): Utilizes the patient assessment instrument to assign patients to one of ninety-seven case-mix groups according to their clinical situation and resource requirements

Inpatient Rehabilitation Validation and Entry (IRVEN): A computerized data-entry system used by inpatient rehabilitation facilities

Inpatient service day: A unit of measure equivalent to the services received by one inpatient during one twenty-four-hour period

In-service education: Training that teaches employees specific skills required to maintain or improve performance, usually internal to an organization

Install base: The number of clients for which a vendor has installed a system, as opposed to the number of clients for which a vendor is in the process of selling a system

Institute of Electrical and Electronics Engineers (IEEE): A national organization that develops standards for hospital system interface transactions, including links between critical care bedside instruments and clinical information systems

Institute of Medicine (IOM): A branch of the National Academy of Sciences whose goal is to advance and distribute scientific knowledge with the mission of improving human health

Institutional review board (IRB): An administrative body that provides oversight for the research studies conducted within a healthcare institution

Instrument: A standardized and uniform way to collect data

Insurance: A purchased contract (policy) according to which the purchaser (insured) is protected from loss by the insurer's agreeing to reimburse for such loss

Insurance certification: The process of determining that the patient has insurance coverage for the treatment that is planned or expected

Insurance code mapping: The methodology that allows a hospital to hold more than one CPT/HCPCS code per chargemaster item

Insured: Individual or entity that purchases healthcare insurance coverage; *See* **certificate holder, member, policyholder,** and **subscriber**

Insurer: An organization that pays healthcare expenses on behalf of its enrollees; *See* **third-party payer**

Integrated delivery system (IDS): A system that combines the financial and clinical aspects of healthcare and uses a group of healthcare providers, selected on the basis of quality and cost management criteria, to furnish comprehensive health services across the continuum of care; *See* **health delivery network, horizontally integrated system, integrated health system, integrated provider organization, integrated services network (ISN),** and **vertically integrated system**

Integrated health system: *See* **integrated delivery system**

Integrated health record format: A system of health record organization in which all of the paper forms are arranged in strict chronological order and mixed with forms created by different departments

Integrated healthcare network: A group of healthcare organizations that collectively provides a full range of coordinated healthcare services ranging from simple preventative care to complex surgical care

Integrated provider organization (IPO): An organization that manages the delivery of healthcare services provided by hospitals, physicians (employees of the IPO), and other healthcare organizations (for example, nursing facilities); *See* **accountable health plan, delivery system, health delivery network, horizontally integrated system, integrated service network, vertically integrated plan,** and **vertically integrated system**

Integrated service network (ISN): *See* **integrated provider organization**

Integrated services digital network (ISDN): A computer system that transmits voice, data, and signaling digitally and with significantly increased bandwidth compared to traditional T-1 lines

112   I   AHIMA

Integration: The complex task of ensuring that all elements and platforms in an information system communicate and act as a uniform entity; or the combination of two or more benefit plans to prevent duplication of benefit payment

Integrative review: *See* **systematic literature review**

Integrity: The state of being whole or unimpaired

Integrity constraints: Limits placed on the data that may be entered into a database

Intellectual capital: The combined knowledge of an organization's employees with respect to operations, processes, history, and culture

Intellectual property: A legal term that refers to creative thoughts that, when they generate a unique solution to a problem, may take on value and thus can become a commodity

Intelligent character recognition (ICR) technology: A method of encoding handwritten, print, or cursive characters and of interpreting the characters as words or the intent of the writer; *See* **gesture recognition technology**

Intelligent document recognition (IDR) technology: Technology that automatically recognizes analog items, such as tangible materials or documents, or recognizes characters or symbols from analog items, enabling the identified data to be quickly, accurately, and automatically entered into digital systems

Intensity of service (IS or IOS): A type of supportive documentation that reflects the diagnostic and therapeutic services for a specified level of care

Intensity-of-service screening criteria: Preestablished standards used to determine the most efficient healthcare setting in which to safely provide needed services

Interactive voice response: An automated call handler that can be configured to automatically dial a log of callers and deliver appointment reminders, lab results, and other information when a person answers the phone

Interactive voice technology (IVT): A communications technology that enables an individual to use a telephone to access information from a computer

Interagency transfer form (W-10): A form that contains sufficient information about a patient to provide continuity of care during transfer or discharge

Interest: The cost of borrowing money; payment to creditors for using money on credit

Interface: The zone between different computer systems across which users want to pass information (for example, a computer program written to exchange information between systems or the graphic display of an application program designed to make the program easier to use)

Interim payment system (IPS): A cost-based reimbursement system that was used until the home health prospective payment system was phased in

Interim period: Any period that represents less than an entire fiscal year

Intermediate care facility: A facility that provides health-related care and services to individuals who do not require the degree of care or treatment that a hospital or a skilled nursing facility provides but who still require medical care and services because of their physical or mental condition

Internal rate of return (IRR): An interest rate that makes the net present value calculation equal zero

Internal validity: An attribute of a study's design that contributes to the accuracy of its findings

International Classification of Diseases for Oncology, Second Edition (ICD-O-2): A classification system used for reporting incidences of malignant disease

International Classification of Diseases, Ninth Revision, Clinical Modification (ICD-9-CM): A classification system used in the United States to report morbidity and mortality information

International Classification of Diseases, Tenth Revision (ICD-10): The newest revision of the disease classification system developed and used by the World Health Organization to track morbidity and mortality information worldwide (not yet adopted by the United States)

International Conference on Harmonization of Technical Requirements for Registration of Pharmaceuticals for Human Use: A joint project established in 1990 that brings together the drug regulatory authorities of the European Union (European Medicines Evaluation Agency), Japan (Ministry of Health and Welfare), and the United States (Food and Drug Administration) as well as representative associations of the pharmaceutical research-based industry in the three regions

International Standards Organization (ISO): An organization that establishes standards in many different areas for many industries so that products and services can be exchanged globally

Internet: An international network of computer servers that provides individual users with communications channels and access to software and information repositories worldwide

Internet browser: A type of client software that facilitates communications among World Wide Web information servers

Internet Engineering Task Force (IETF): A group that reviews and issues Internet standards

Internet protocol (IP) telephony: A type of communications technology that allows people to initiate real-time calls through the Internet instead of the public telephone system; *See* **voiceover IP (VoIP)**

Internet service provider (ISP): A company that provides connections to the Internet

Interoperability: The ability, generally by adoption of standards, of systems to work together

Interpersonal skills: One of the three managerial skill categories that includes skills in communicating and relating effectively to others

Interpreter: A type of communications technology that converts high-level language statements into machine language one at a time

Interrater reliability: A measure of a research instrument's consistency in data collection when used by different abstractors

Interrogatories: Discovery devices consisting of a set of written questions given to a party, witness, or other person who has information needed in a legal case

Interrupted stay case: A rehabilitation stay interrupted by a single admission to an acute care hospital

Interval data: A type of data that represents observations that can be measured on an evenly distributed scale beginning at a point other than true zero

Interval level data: Data with a defined unit of measure, no true zero point, and equal intervals between successive values; *See* **ratio level data**

Interval note: Health record documentation that describes the patient's course between two closely related hospitalizations directed toward the treatment of the same complaint

Intervention: 1. A clinical manipulation, treatment, or therapy 2. A generic term used by researchers to mean an act of some kind

Interview guide: A list of written questions to be asked during an interview

Interview survey: A type of research instrument with which the members of the population being studied are asked questions and respond orally

Intrahospital transfer: A change in medical care unit, medical staff unit, or responsible physician during hospitalization

Intranet: A private information network that is similar to the Internet and whose servers are located inside a firewall or security barrier so that the general public cannot gain access to information housed within the network

Intraoperative anesthesia record: Health record documentation that describes the entire surgical process from the time the operation began until the patient left the operating room

Intrarater reliability: A measure of a research instrument's reliability in which the same person repeating the test will get reasonably similar findings

Intuition: Unconscious decision making based on extensive experience in similar situations

Inventor: A role in organizational innovation that requires idea generation

Inventory: Goods on hand and available to sell, presumably within a year (a business cycle)

Inverse relationship: *See* **negative relationship**

IOM: *See* **Institute of Medicine**

IOS: *See* **intensity of service**

IPA: *See* **independent practice association**

IPF: *See* **inpatient psychiatric facility**

IPFPPS: *See* **inpatient psychiatric facility PPS**

IPO: *See* **independent practice organization**

IPO: *See* **integrated provider organization**

IPS: *See* **interim payment system**

IP telephony: *See* **Internet protocol telephony**

IRB: *See* **institutional review board**

IRF: *See* **inpatient rehabilitative facility**

IRFPPS: *See* **inpatient rehabilitation facility PPS**

IRR: *See* **internal rate of return**

IRVEN: *See* **Inpatient Rehabilitation Validation and Entry**

IS: *See* **information system**

IS: *See* **intensity of service**

IS-A relationships: Relationships that link concepts within a hierarchy; in SNOMED CT, concepts are always related by IS-A relationship to the concept directly above them

IS department: *See* **information systems department**

ISDN: *See* **integrated services digital network**

ISN: *See* **integrated service network**

ISO: *See* **International Standards Organization** and **United Nations International Standards Organization**

ISO 9000: An internationally agreed-upon set of generic standards for quality management established by the International Standards Organization

ISP: *See* **Internet service provider**

ISS: *See* **injury severity score**

IS/SI criteria: *See* **intensity-of-service screening criteria; severity-of-illness screening criteria**

Issue log: A form of documentation that describes the questions, concerns, and problems that must be solved in order for a task to be completed

IT: *See* **information technology**

Item description: An explanation of a service or supply listed in the chargemaster

IT professional: *See* **information technology professional**

IT strategy: *See* **information technology strategy**

IVT: *See* **interactive voice technology**

J

JCAHO: *See* **Joint Commission on Accreditation of Healthcare Organization**

JIT: *See* **just-in-time training**

Job classification: 1. A method of job evaluation that compares a written position description with the written descriptions of various classification grades 2. A method used by the federal government to grade jobs

Job description: A list of a job's duties, reporting relationships, working conditions, and responsibilities; *See* **position description**

Job evaluation: The process of applying predefined compensable factors to jobs to determine their relative worth

Job procedure: A structured, action-oriented list of sequential steps involved in carrying out a specific job or solving a problem

Job ranking: A method of job evaluation that arranges jobs in a hierarchy on the basis of each job's importance to the organization, with the most important jobs listed at the top of the hierarchy and the least important jobs listed at the bottom

Job rotation: A work design in which workers are shifted periodically among different tasks

Job sharing: A work schedule in which two or more individuals share the tasks of one full-time or one full-time-equivalent position

Job specification: A list of a job's required education, skills, knowledge, abilities, personal qualifications, and physical requirements

Joint Commission on Accreditation of Healthcare Organizations (JCAHO): A private, not-for-profit organization that evaluates and accredits hospitals and other healthcare organizations on the basis of predefined performance standards

Joint venture: The result of two or more companies investing together in a mutually beneficial project

Journal entry: An accounting representation of a financial transaction or transfer of amounts between accounts that contains at least one debit and one credit and in which the dollar value of the debits and the credits is the same

Judge-made law: *See* **common law**

Judicial decision: A ruling handed down by a court to settle a legal dispute

Jurisdiction: The power and authority of a court to hear and decide specific types of cases

Justice: The impartial administration of policies or laws that takes into consideration the competing interests and limited resources of the individuals or groups involved

Just-in-time training (JIT): Training provided anytime, anyplace, and just when it is needed

Key: In cryptography, a secret value used to encrypt and decrypt messages; in a symmetric cryptographic algorithm, only one key is needed to encrypt and decrypt a message, but in an asymmetric algorithm, two keys are needed; *See* **cryptography; private key; public key**

Key attributes: Common fields (attributes) within a relational database that are used to link tables to one another

Key field: An explanatory notation that uniquely identifies each row in a database table; *See* **primary key**

K-nearest neighbor (K-NN): A classic technique used to discover associations and sequences when the data attributes are numeric

K-NN: *See* **K-nearest neighbor**

Knowledge: The information, understanding, and experience that give individuals the power to make informed decisions

Knowledge assets: Assets that are the sources of knowledge for an organization (for example, printed documents, unwritten rules, work flows, customer knowledge, data in databases and spreadsheets, and the human expertise, know-how, and tacit knowledge within the minds of the organization's workforce)

Knowledge base: A database that not only manages raw data but also integrates them with information from various reference works; *See* **data repository**

Knowledge-based assets: Assets that are the sources of knowledge for an organization (for example, printed documents; unwritten rules; work flows; customer knowledge; data in databases and spreadsheets; and the human expertise, know-how, and tacit knowledge within the minds of the organization's workforce)

Knowledge management: 1. The process by which data are acquired and transformed into information through the application of context, which in turn provides understanding   2. A management philosophy that promotes an integrated and collaborative approach to the process of information asset creation, capture, organization, access, and use

Knowledge production: Involves the creation of knowledge through collection, generation, synthesis, and identification and organization of knowledge through codification, storage, packaging, and coordination

Knowledge refinement: Consists of evaluation, reflection, adaptation, and sustainability of knowledge

Knowledge sources: Various types of reference material and expert information that are compiled in a manner accessible for integration with patient care information to improve the quality and cost-effectiveness of healthcare provision

Knowledge use: Consists of distribution, sharing, application, and integration of knowledge

Knowledge worker: An employee who improves his or her performance by sharing his or her experience and expertise with other employees

Kolb's "Learning Loop": A theory of experiential learning involving four interrelated steps: concrete experiences, observation and reflection, formation of abstract concepts and theories, and testing new implications of theory in new situations

Labeler Code: The first segment of the National Drug Code (NDC); assigned by FDA to a firm

Labor and delivery record: Health record documentation that takes the place of an operative report for patients who gave birth in the obstetrics department of an acute care hospital

Labor organization: *See* **union**

Labor relations: Human resources management activities associated with unions and collective bargaining

Laggards: A category of adopters of change who are very reluctant to accept proposed changes and may resist transition

LAN: *See* **local-area network**

Language translator: A software system that translates a program written in a particular computer language into a language that other types of computers can understand

Large urban area: An urban area with a population of more than one million

Late enrollee: Individual who does not enroll in a group healthcare plan at the first opportunity, but enrolls later if the plan has a general open enrollment period

Late majority: A category of adopters of change who change only in response to peer, authority, or economic pressure

LCMS: *See* **Learning Content Management System**

Leader-member exchange: a leadership theory in which a group that shows high potential (the "in-group") is given opportunities for special assignments in exchange for their loyalty and extra work; *See* **vertical dyad linkage**

Leader–member relations: A situation in contingency theory describing how well the leader is liked, respected, and followed

Leadership grid: A leadership model proposed by Blake and Mouton and based on a grid measure of concern for people and production

Leading: One of the four management functions in which people are directed and motivated to achieve goals

Learning Content Management System (LCMS): Training software development tools that assist with management, sharing, and reuse of course content

Learning curve: The time required to acquire and apply certain skills so that new levels of productivity and/or performance exceed prelearning levels (productivity often is inversely related to the learning curve)

Learning Management System (LMS): A software application that assists with managing and tracking learners and learning events and collating data on learner progress

Learning organization: An organization in which the emphasis is on acquiring and sharing business knowledge along with delivering information quickly, clearly, and visually to everyone within the organization

Least-Preferred Coworker Scale (LPC): A bipolar scale used by Fiedler to measure task–relationship orientation in contingency theory

Leave of absence: The authorized absence of an inpatient from a hospital or other facility for a specified period of time occurring after admission and prior to discharge

Lecture: A one-way method of delivering education through speaking in which the teacher delivers the speech and the student listens

Legacy system: A type of computer system that uses older technology but may still perform optimally

Legal entity: The form of a business organization recognized by law, for example, a sole proprietorship, a partnership, or a corporation

Legislative law: *See* **statutory law**

Length of stay (LOS): The total number of patient days for an inpatient episode, calculated by subtracting the date of admission from the date of discharge

Level of service: 1. The relative intensity of services given when a physician provides one-on-one services for a patient (such as minimal, brief, limited, or intermediate) 2. The relative intensity of services provided by a healthcare facility (for example, tertiary care)

Leveraged buyout: The result of the stock of a publicly traded company being purchased, often by its own management, with a large amount of debt and the company's assets as collateral for the loan

Lexicon: 1. The vocabulary used in a language or a subject area or by a particular speaker or group of speakers

2. A collection of words or terms and their meanings for a particular domain, used in healthcare for drug terms

Liability: 1. A legal obligation or responsibility that may have financial repercussions if not fulfilled   2. An amount owed by an individual or organization to another individual or organization

Liability files policy: A policy that outlines procedures for limiting access to, and maintaining the security of, information related to liability cases

Licensed practitioner: An individual at any level of professional specialization who requires a public license or certification to engage in patient care

Licensure: The legal authority or formal permission from authorities to carry on certain activities that by law or regulation require such permission (applicable to institutions as well as individuals)

Licensure requirements: Criteria healthcare providers must meet in order to gain and retain state licensure to provide specific services

Life cycle costs: The costs of a project beyond its purchase price, for example, setup costs, training costs, and so on, as well as costs incurred throughout the project's estimated useful life

Likert scale: An ordinal scaling and summated rating technique for measuring the attitudes of respondents; a measure that records level of agreement or disagreement along a progression of categories, usually five (five-point scale), often administered in the form of a questionnaire

Limitation: Qualification or other specification that reduces or restricts the extent of a healthcare benefit

Limiting charge: A percentage limit on physicians' fees that nonparticipating providers may bill Medicare beneficiaries above the fee schedule amount

Linear programming: An operational management technique that uses mathematical formulas to determine the optimal way to allocate resources for a project

Line authority: The authority to manage subordinates and to have them report back, based on relationships illustrated in an organizational chart

Line graph: A graphic technique used to illustrate the relationship between continuous measurements; consists of a line drawn to connect a series of points on an arithmetic scale; often used to display time trends

Line item: A service- or item-specific detail of a reimbursement claim

Linkage analysis: A technique used to explore and examine relationships among a large number of variables of different types

Linux: A freeware operating system similar to UNIX

Liquidity: The speed with which an asset can be converted into cash

Literature review: A systematic and critical investigation of the important information about a topic; may include books, journal articles, theses, dissertations, periodicals, technical and research reports, proceedings of conferences, audiovisual media, and electronic media; *See* **systematic literature review**

Litigation: A civil lawsuit or contest in court

Living arrangement: A data element that denotes whether the patient lives alone or with others

Living will: A directive that allows an individual to describe in writing the type of healthcare that he or she would or would not wish to receive

LMRPs: *See* **local medical review policies**

LMS: *See* **Learning Management System**

Local-area network (LAN): A network that connects multiple computer devices via continuous cable within a relatively small geographic area

Local Codes: Also known as HCPCS Level III Codes, these codes were developed by local Medicare and/or Medicaid carriers and were eliminated December 31, 2003 to comply with HIPAA

Local medical review policies (LMRPs): Documents that define Medicare coverage of outpatient services via lists of diagnoses defined as medically reasonable and necessary for the services provided

Location or address of encounter: The full address and nine-digit zip code for the location at which outpatient care was received from the healthcare practitioner of record

Logical: 1. A user's view of the way data or systems are organized (for example, a file that is a collection of data stored together) 2. The opposite of physical

Logical data model: The second level of data model that is drawn according to the type of database to be developed

Logical Observation Identifiers, Names and Codes (LOINC): A database protocol developed by the Regenstrief Institute for Health Care aimed at standardizing laboratory and clinical codes for use in clinical care, outcomes management, and research

LOINC: *See* **Logical Observation Identifiers, Names and Codes**

Longitudinal: A type of time frame for research studies during which data are collected from the same participants at multiple points in time

Longitudinal health record: A permanent, coordinated patient record of significant information listed in chronological order and maintained across time, ideally from birth to death

Long-term care: Healthcare services provided in a non-acute care setting to chronically ill, aged, disabled, or mentally handicapped individuals

Long-term care facility: A healthcare organization that provides medical, nursing, rehabilitation, and subacute care services to residents who need continual supervision and/or assistance

LOS: *See* **length of stay**

Loss prevention: A risk management strategy that includes developing and revising policies and procedures that are both facilitywide and department specific

Loss reduction: A component of a risk management program that encompasses techniques used to manage events or claims that already have taken place

Low-birth-weight neonate: Any newborn baby, regardless of gestational age, whose weight at birth is less than 2500 grams

Low-utilization payment adjustment (LUPA): An alternative (reduced) payment made to home health agencies instead of the home health resource group reimbursement rate when a patient receives fewer than four home care visits during a sixty-day episode

Low-volume hospital: A hospital with fewer than 5000 outpatient visits per year

Lower courts: The lowest level of the U.S. judicial system, where state and local criminal and civil cases are tried; *See* **trial courts**

LPC: *See* **Least-Preferred Coworker Scale**

LTCH: *See* **inpatient long term care hospital**

Lumper Vocabulary: A medical vocabulary that does not attempt to provide names for all things and activities, but rather provides codes that combine multiple concepts for a specific purpose; for example, LOINC gathers concepts into a code that can be "exploded" into components when needed

LUPA: *See* **low-utilization payment adjustment**

M

AC: *See* **maximum allowable charges**

Machine language: Binary codes made up of zeroes and ones that computers use directly to represent precise storage locations and operations

Machine learning: An area of computer science that studies algorithms and computer programs that improve employee performance on some task by exposure to a training or learning experience

Macro virus: A type of computer virus that infects Microsoft Word applications by inserting unwanted words or phrases

Mainframe computer: A computer architecture built with a single central processing unit to which dumb terminals and/or personal computers are connected

Main provider: A provider that either creates or owns another entity in order to deliver additional healthcare services under its name, ownership, and financial and administrative control

Maintenance and evaluation phase: The fourth and final phase of the systems development life cycle that helps to ensure that adequate technical support staff and resources are available to maintain or support the new system

Major diagnostic category (MDC): Under diagnosis-related groups (DRGs), one of twenty-five categories based on single or multiple organ systems into which all diseases and disorders relating to that system are classified; *See* **diagnosis-related group**

Major medical insurance: Prepaid healthcare benefits that include a high limit for most types of medical expenses and usually require a large deductible and sometimes place limits on coverage and charges (for example, room and board); *See* **catastrophic coverage**

Major teaching hospital: A hospital that provides clinical education to one hundred or more resident physicians

Managed behavioral healthcare organization (MBHO): A type of healthcare organization that delivers and manages all aspects of behavioral healthcare or the payment for care by limiting providers of care, discounting payment to providers of care, and/or limiting access to care

Managed care: 1. Payment method in which the third party payer has implemented some provisions to control the costs of healthcare while maintaining quality care 2. Systematic merger of clinical, financial, and administrative processes to manage access, cost, and quality of healthcare

Managed care organization (MCO): A type of healthcare organization that delivers medical care and manages all aspects of the care or the payment for care by limiting providers of care, discounting payment to providers of care, and/or limiting access to care

Managed fee-for-service reimbursement: A healthcare plan that implements utilization controls (prospective and retrospective review of healthcare services) for reimbursement under traditional fee-for-service insurance plans

Management: The process of planning, organizing, and leading an organization's activities

Management by objectives (MBO): A management approach that defines target objectives for organizing work and comparing performance against those objectives

Management functions: Traditionally, the tasks of planning, organizing, directing, coordinating, and controlling

Management information system (MIS): A computer-based system that provides information to a healthcare organization's managers for use in making decisions that affect a variety of day-to-day activities

Management services organization (MSO): An organization, usually owned by a group of physicians or a hospital, that provides administrative and support services to one or more physician group practices or small hospitals

Managerial accounting: The development, implementation, and analysis of systems that track financial transactions for management control purposes, including both budget systems and cost analysis systems

Many-to-many relationship: The concept (occurring only in a conceptual model) that multiple instances of an entity may be associated with multiple instances of another entity

Mapping: Creation of a cross map that links the content from one classification or terminology scheme to another

Marital status: The marital state of the patient at the start of care (for example, married, living together, not living together, never married, widowed, divorced, separated, or unknown/not stated)

Market basket index: A device used in the home health prospective payment system to reflect changes over time in the prices of an appropriate mix of goods and services and to develop the national sixty-day episode payment rates

Marketing: The process of issuing a communication about a product or service with the purpose of encouraging recipients of the communication to purchase or use the product or service

Market value: The price at which something can be bought or sold on the open market

Mark sense technology: Technology that detects the presence or absence of handmarked characters on analog documents; used for processing questionnaires, surveys, and tests, such as filled-in circles by Number 2 pencils on exam forms

MARS: *See* **medication administration records**

Massachusetts General Hospital Utility Multiprogramming System: *See* **M technology**

Massed training: An educational technique that requires learning a large amount of material at one time

Master patient index (MPI): A list or database created and maintained by a healthcare facility to record the name and identification number of every patient who has ever been admitted or treated in the facility; *See* **master population index** and **master person index**

Master person index: *See* **master patient index**

Master population index: *See* **master patient index**

Master resident index: A listing or database that a long-term care facility keeps to record all the residents who have ever been admitted or treated there

Master resident index maintenance policy: A policy that outlines procedures on the maintenance of the master resident index and the steps to take to verify and cross-check all entries

Matching: A concept that enables decision makers to look at expenses and revenues in the same period to measure the organization's income performance

Matching expenses: The costs that are recorded during the same period as the related revenue

Materiality: The significance of a dollar amount based on predetermined criteria

Maternal death: The death of any woman, from any cause, related to or aggravated by pregnancy or its management (regardless of duration or site of pregnancy), but not from accidental or incidental causes

Maternal death rate: For a hospital, the total number of maternal deaths directly related to pregnancy for a given time period divided by the total number of obstetrical discharges for the same time period; for a community, the total number of deaths attributed to maternal conditions during a given time period in a specific geographic area divided by the total number of live births for the same time period in the same area

Maximum allowable charges (MAC): The maximum charges allowed for a service rendered

Maximum out-of-pocket cost: Specific amount, in a certain time frame such as one year, beyond which all covered healthcare services for that policyholder are covered by the insurer

MBHO: *See* **managed behavioral healthcare organization**

MBO: *See* **management by objectives**

MCO: *See* **managed care organization**

MDC: *See* **major diagnostic category**

MDDBMS: *See* **multidimensional database management system**

MDS: *See* **Minimum Data Set**

MDS-PAC: *See* **Minimum Data Set for Post Acute Care**

MDS processing policy: A policy that applies when health record personnel are included in the MDS data entry or submission of the MDS data

MDS 2.0: *See* **Minimum Data Set for Long-Term Care, Version 2.0**

Mean: A measure of central tendency that is determined by calculating the arithmetic average of the observations in a frequency distribution

Measure: The quantifiable data about a function or process

Measurement: The systematic process of data collection, repeated over time or at a single point in time

Measures of central tendency: The typical or average numbers that are descriptive of the entire collection of data for a specific population

MedDra: *See* **Medical Dictionary for Regulatory Activities**

Media controls: The policies and procedures that govern the receipt and removal of hardware, software, and computer media (such as disks and tapes) in to and out of the organization

Median: A measure of central tendency that shows the midpoint of a frequency distribution when the observations have been arranged in order from lowest to highest

Medicaid: An entitlement program that oversees medical assistance for individuals and families with low incomes and limited resources; jointly funded between state and federal governments

Medical audits: *See* **medical care evaluation studies**

Medical care evaluation studies: Audits required by the Medicare *Conditions of Participation* that dictate the use of screening criteria with evaluation by diagnosis and/or procedure; *See* **medical audits**

Medical care unit: An assemblage of inpatient beds (or newborn bassinets), related facilities, and assigned personnel that provide service to a defined and limited class of patients according to their particular medical care needs

Medical classification system: A method of arranging related diseases and conditions into groups to be reported as quantitative data for statistical purposes

Medical consultation: *See* **consultation**

Medical Data Interchange Standard (MEDIX): A set of hospital system interface transaction standards developed by the Institute of Electrical and Electronic Engineers

Medical Dictionary for Regulatory Activities (MedDRA): A vocabulary that has been developed as a pragmatic, clinically validated medical terminology with an emphasis on ease-of-use data entry, retrieval, analysis, and display, with a suitable balance between sensitivity and specificity, within the regulatory environment; applicable to all phases of drug development and the health effects of devices

Medical emergency: Severe injury or illness (including pain); definition depends upon healthcare insurer

Medical foundation: Multi-purpose, non-profit service organization for physicians and other healthcare providers at the local and county level; as managed care organizations, medical foundations have established preferred provider organization, exclusive provider organizations, and management service organizations, with emphases on freedom of choice and preservation of the physician-patient relationship

Medical Group Management Association (MGMA): A national organization composed of individuals actively engaged in the business management of medical groups consisting of three or more physicians in medical practice

Medical history: A record of the information provided by a patient to his or her physician to explain the patient's chief complaint, present and past illnesses, and personal and family medical problems; includes a description of the physician's review of systems

Medical informatics: A field of information science concerned with the management of data and information used to diagnose, treat, cure, and prevent disease through the application of computers and computer technologies

Medical information bus (MIB): The part of the IEEE standard that provides open integration standards for connecting electronic patient-monitoring devices with information systems

Medical Literature, Analysis, and Retrieval System Online (MEDLINE): A computerized, online database in the bibliographic Medical Literature Analysis and Retrieval System (MEDLARS) of the National Library of Medicine

Medically needy option: An option in the Medicaid program that allows states to extend eligibility to persons who would be eligible for Medicaid under one of the mandatory or optional groups but whose income and/or resources fall above the eligibility level set by their state

Medical malpractice: The professional liability of healthcare providers in the delivery of patient care

Medical necessity: The likelihood that a proposed healthcare service will have a reasonable beneficial effect on the patient's physical condition and quality of life at a specific point in his or her illness or lifetime

Medical nomenclature: A recognized system of preferred terminology for naming disease processes

Medical Outcomes Study Short-Form Health Survey: A patient survey that reflects the patients' disease and symptom intensity to characterize the total burden of the disease

Medical record: *See* **health record**

Medical record administrator: *See* **health information management professional**

Medical records department: *See* **health information services department**

Medical record technician: *See* **health information management professional**

Medical research: *See* **clinical research**

Medical savings account (MSA) plans: Plans that provide benefits after a single, high deductible has been met whereby Medicare makes an annual deposit to the MSA and the beneficiary is expected to use the money in the MSA to pay for medical expenses below the annual deductible

Medical service bureaus: Organized groups of physicians who were paid by employers to provide healthcare services to their employees during the early 1900s

Medical specialties: A group of clinical specialties that concentrates on the provision of nonsurgical care by physicians who have received advanced training in internal medicine, pediatrics, cardiology, endocrinology, psychiatry, oncology, nephrology, neurology, pulmonology, gastroenterology, dermatology, radiology, or nuclear medicine

Medical staff: A formal organization of physicians (or other professionals such as dentists) with the delegated authority and responsibility to maintain proper standards of medical care and to plan for continued betterment of that care

Medical staff bylaws: A collection of guidelines adopted by a hospital's medical staff to govern its business conduct and the rights and responsibilities of its members

Medical staff classifications: Categories of clinical practice privileges assigned to individual practitioners on the basis of their qualifications; *See* **medical staff privileges**

Medical staff organization (MSO): A self-governing entity that operates as a responsible extension of the governing body and exists for the purpose of providing patient care

Medical staff unit: One of the departments, divisions, or specialties into which the organized medical staff of a hospital is divided

Medical Subjects Heading database (MeSH): The National Library of Medicine's (NLM's) controlled vocabulary for indexing journal articles

Medical transcription: The conversion of verbal medical reports dictated by healthcare providers into written form for inclusion in patients' health records

Medical transcriptionist: A medical language specialist who types or word-processes information dictated by providers

Medical vocabulary: *See* **clinical vocabulary**

Medicare: A federally-funded health program established in 1965 to assist with the medical care costs of Americans sixty-five years of age and older as well as other individuals entitled to Social Security benefits owing to their disabilities

Medicare Advantage (Part C): Optional managed care plan for Medicare beneficiaries who are entitled to Part A, enrolled in Part B, and live in an area with a plan; types include health maintenance organization, point-of-service plan, preferred provider organization, and provider-sponsored organization; formerly **Medicare+Choice**

Medicare+Choice: former name of **Medicare Advantage**

Medicare *Conditions of Participation* (COP): A publication that describes the requirements that institutional providers (such as hospitals, skilled nursing facilities, and home health agencies) must meet to receive reimbursement for services provided to Medicare beneficiaries

Medicare discharge: The status of Medicare patients who are formally released from a hospital, die in a hospital, or are transferred to another hospital or unit excluded from the prospective payment system

Medicare economic index (MEI): An index used by the Medicare program to update physician fee levels in relation to annual changes in the general economy for inflation, productivity, and changes in specific health-sector expense factors including malpractice, personnel costs, rent, and other expenses

Medicare fee schedule (MFS): A feature of the resource-based relative value system that includes a complete list of the payments Medicare makes to physicians and other providers

Medicare Part A: *See* **hospitalization insurance**

Medicare Part B: *See* **supplemental medical insurance**

Medicare Part C: *See* **Medicare Advantage**

Medicare prospective payment system: *See* **acute care prospective payment system, home health prospective payment system, outpatient prospective payment system,** and **skilled nursing facility prospective payment system**

Medicare Provider Analysis and Review (MEDPAR) database system: A database containing information submitted by fiscal intermediaries that is used by the Office of the Inspector General to identify suspicious billing and charge practices

Medicare Provider Analysis and Review (MEDPAR) File: A collection of data from reimbursement claims submitted to the Medicare program by acute care hospitals and skilled nursing facilities that is used to evaluate the quality and effectiveness of the care being provided

Medicare-required assessment: A Minimum Data Set for Long-Term Care completed solely for the purpose of Medicare rate setting for skilled nursing facilities

Medicare summary notice: A summary sent to the patient from Medicare that summarizes all services provided over a period of time with an explanation of benefits provided

Medicare volume performance standard (MVPS): A goal for the annual rate of growth in Part B expenditures for physicians' services

Medication administration records (MARs): Tools used to capture the delivery of drugs to residents

Medication record: Health record documentation that lists all of the medications administered to a patient while he or she is on a nursing unit

Medications prescribed: Descriptions (including, where possible, the national drug code, dosage, strength, and total amount prescribed) of all medications prescribed or provided by the healthcare practitioner at the encounter (for outpatients) or given on discharge to the patient (for inpatients)

Medigap: A private insurance policy that supplements Medicare coverage

MEDIX: *See* **Medical Dictionary for Regulatory Activities**

MEDLINE: *See* **Medical Literature, Analysis, and Retrieval System Online**

MEDPAR database system: *See* **Medicare Provider Analysis and Review database system**

MEDPAR File: *See* **Medicare Provider Analysis and Review File**

MEI: *See* **Medicare economic index**

Member: Individual or entity that purchases healthcare insurance coverage *See* **certificate holder, insured, policyholder,** and **subscriber**

Member months: The total membership each month accumulated for a given time period (for example, one hundred members serviced each month for six months equals six hundred member months)

Mental ability tests: Tests that assess the reasoning capabilities of individuals

Mentoring: A type of employee coaching in which an individual in the beginning stages of his or her career is matched with a more experienced person who serves as an advisor

Merger: A business situation where two or more companies combine, but one of them continues to exist as a legal, business entity, while the others cease to exist legally and their assets and liabilities become part of the continuing company

MeSH: *See* **Medical Subjects Heading database**

Message format standards: *See* **data exchange standards**

Messaging standards: *See* **transmission standards**

Meta-analysis: A specialized form of systematic literature review that involves the statistical analysis of a large collection of results from individual studies for the purpose of integrating the studies' findings

Metadata: Descriptive data that characterize other data to create a clearer understanding of their meaning and to achieve greater reliability and quality of information

Method: 1. A way of performing an action or task   2. A strategy used by a researcher to collect, analyze, and present data

MFS: *See* **Medicare fee schedule**

MGMA: *See* **Medical Group Management Association**

MIB: *See* **medical information bus**

Microcomputer: A personal computer characterized by its relatively small size and fast processing speed

Microcontroller: A small, low-cost computer installed in an appliance or electronic device to perform a specific task or program

Microfilming: A photographic process that reduces an original paper document into a small image on film to save storage space

Middle managers: The individuals in an organization who oversee the operation of a broad scope of functions at the departmental level or who oversee defined product or service lines

Middleware: A bridge between two applications or the software equivalent of an interface

Midnight rule: A Medicare regulation that states that the day preceding a leave of absence becomes a nonbillable day for Medicare purposes when a Part A beneficiary takes a leave of absence and is not present in the skilled nursing facility at midnight

Midsize computer: *See* **minicomputer**

Migration path: A series of steps required to move from one situation to another

Milestone budget: A type of budget without a fixed 12 month calendar in which cost is determined and budget allocation is established for the next period as events are completed; *See* **program budget**

MIME: *See* **multipurpose Internet mail extension**

Minicomputer: A small, mainframe computer; *See* **midsize computer**

Minimum Data Set (MDS): The instrument specified by the Centers for Medicare and Medicaid Services that requires nursing facilities (both Medicare certified and/or Medicaid certified) to conduct a comprehensive, accurate, standardized, reproducible assessment of each resident's functional capacity

Minimum Data Set for Long-Term Care, Version 2.0 (MDS 2.0): A federally mandated standard assessment form that Medicare- and/or Medicaid-certified nursing facilities must use to collect demographic and clinical data on nursing home residents

Minimum Data Set for Post Acute Care (MDS-PAC): A patient-centered assessment instrument that must be completed for every Medicare patient and emphasizes a patient's care needs instead of provider characteristics

Minimum necessary standard: A stipulation of the HIPAA privacy rule that requires healthcare facilities and other covered entities to make reasonable efforts to limit the patient-identifiable information they disclose to the least amount required to accomplish the intended purpose for which the information was requested

Minor: An infant or person under the age of legal competence

MIS: *See* **management information system**

Miscellaneous Codes: National codes used when a supplier is submitting a bill for an item or service and there is no existing national code that describes the item or service being billed

Misdemeanor: A crime that is less serious than a felony

Mission statement: A short description of an organization's or group's general purpose for existing

Mixed costs: Costs that are part variable and part fixed

m-learning: Mobile learning; the application of e-learning to mobile computing devices and wireless networks; *See* **e-learning**

Mode: A measure of central tendency that consists of the most frequent observation in a frequency distribution

Model: The representation of a theory in a visual format, on a smaller scale, or with objects

Modifier: A two-digit numeric code listed after a procedure code that indicates that a service was altered in some way from the stated CPT descriptor without changing the definition; also used to enhance a code narrative to describe the circumstances of each procedure or service and how it individually applies to a patient

MOLAP: *See* **multidimensional online analytical processing**

Morality: A composite of the personal values concerning what is considered right or wrong in a specific cultural group

Morbidity: A term referring to the state of being diseased (including illness, injury, or deviation from normal health); the number of sick persons or cases of disease in relationship to a specific population

Morphology axis: Structural change in tissue

Mortality: 1. A term referring to the incidence of death in a specific population   2. The loss of subjects during the course of a clinical research study; *See* **attrition**

Most significant diagnosis: *See* **principal diagnosis**

Motion video: A medium for storing, manipulating, and displaying moving images in a format, such as frames, that can be presented on a computer monitor; *See* **frame data** and **streaming video**

Motivation: The drive to accomplish a task

Movement diagram: A chart depicting the location of furniture and equipment in a work area and showing the usual flow of individuals or materials as they progress through the work area

MPI: *See* **master patient index**

MSA plans: *See* **medical savings account plans**

MSO: *See* **management service organization**

M technology: An operating system developed more than twenty-five years ago and still widely used today, which uses "write once, run anywhere" characteristics; formerly Massachusetts General Hospital Utility Multiprogramming System (MUMPS)

Multiaxial system: A system that can classify an entity in several different ways

Multidimensional analysis: Simultaneous analysis of data from multiple dimensions using different data elements

Multidimensional database management system (MDDBMS): A database management system specifically designed to handle data organized into a data structure with numerous dimensions

Multidimensional data structure: A structure whereby data are organized according to the dimensions associated with them

Multidimensional online analytical processing (MOLAP): A data access methodology that is coupled tightly with a multidimensional database management system to allow the user to perform business analyses

Multimedia: The combination of free-text, raster or vector graphics, sound, and/or motion video/frame data

Multipurpose Internet mail extension (MIME): A standard developed for the transmission of nontextual information via e-mail

Multiservice contractor: A small company that provides coding services or services related to coding

Multivariate: A term used in reference to research studies that means that many variables were involved

Multivoting technique: A decision-making method for determining group consensus on the prioritization of issues or solutions

MUMPS: *See* **Massachusetts General Hospital Utility Multiprogramming System**

Municipal ordinance/code: A rule established by a local branch of government such as a town, city, or county

MVPS: *See* **Medicare volume performance standard**

N

NAACCR: *See* **North American Association of Central Cancer Registries**

NACHRI classification: *See* **National Association of Children's Hospitals and Related Institutions classifications**

NAHQ: *See* **National Association of Healthcare Quality**

NAR: *See* **nursing assessment record**

National Association of Children's Hospitals and Related Institutions (NACHRI) classification: A classification of congenital and chronic health conditions that uses disease progression factors for case-mix analysis

National Association of Healthcare Quality (NAHQ): An organization devoted to advancing the profession of healthcare quality improvement through its accreditation program

National Centers for Health Statistics (NCHS): The federal agency responsible for collecting and disseminating information on health services utilization and the health status of the population in the United States

National Committee for Quality Assurance (NCQA): A private not-for-profit accreditation organization whose mission is to evaluate and report on the quality of managed care organizations in the United States

National Committee on Vital and Health Statistics (NCVHS): A public policy advisory board that recommends policy to the National Center for Health Statistics and other health-related federal programs

National conversion factor (CF): A mathematical factor used to convert relative value units into monetary payments for services provided to Medicare beneficiaries

National Correct Coding Initiative: A series of code edits on Medicare Part B claims

National Council on Prescription Drug Programs (NCPDP): An organization that develops standards for exchanging prescription and payment information

National Drug Codes (NDC): Codes that serve as product identifiers for human drugs, currently limited to prescription drugs and a few selected over-the-counter products

National Guideline Clearinghouse (NGC): A partnership among the Agency for Healthcare Research and Quality, the American Medical Association, and the American Association of Health Plans that allows free online access to its clinical guidelines

National Health Care Survey: A national public health survey that contains data abstracted manually from a sample of acute care hospitals or from discharged inpatient records or that are obtained from state or other discharge databases

National Information Infrastructure—Health Information Network Program (NII–HIN): A national quasi-governmental organization that provides oversight of all healthcare information standards in the United States

National Library of Medicine (NLM): The world's largest medical library and a branch of the National Institutes of Health

National Permanent Codes: These HCPCS level II codes provide a standard coding system that is managed by private and public insurers and provide a stable environment for claims submission and processing

National Practitioner Data Bank (NPDB): A data bank established by the federal government through the 1986 Health Care Quality Improvement Act that contains information on professional review actions taken against physicians and other licensed healthcare practitioners, which healthcare organizations are required to check as part of the credentialing process

National provider file (NPF): A file developed by the Centers for Medicare and Medicaid Services that includes all healthcare providers, including nonphysicians, and sites of care

National provider identifier (NPI): An eight-character alphanumeric identifier used to identify individual healthcare providers for Medicare billing purposes

National standard per-visit rates: Rates for six home health disciplines based on historical claims data that are used in the payment of low-utilization payment adjustments and the calculation of outliers

National Uniform Billing Committee (NUBC): The national group responsible for identifying data elements and designing the CMS-1500

National Uniform Claim Committee (NUCC): The national group that replaced the Uniform Claim Form Task Force in 1995 and developed a standard data set to be used in the transmission of noninstitutional provider claims to and from third-party payers

National Vaccine Advisory Committee (NVAC): A national advisory group that supports the director of the National Vaccine Program

National Vital Statistics System (NVSS): A federal agency responsible for the collection of official vital statistics for the United States

Naturalism: A philosophy of research that assumes that multiple contextual truths exist and bias is always present; *See* **qualitative approach**

Naturalistic observation: A type of nonparticipant observation in which researchers observe certain behaviors and events as they occur naturally

Natural language: A fifth-generation computer programming language that uses human language to give people a more natural connection with computers

Natural language processing technology: The extraction of unstructured or structured medical word data, which are then translated into diagnostic or procedural codes for clinical and administrative applications

NB: *See* **newborn**

NCHS: *See* **National Centers for Health Statistics**

NCPDP: *See* **National Council on Prescription Drug Programs**

NCQA: *See* **National Committee for Quality Assurance**

NCR: *See* **no carbon required**

NCVHS: *See* **National Committee on Vital and Health Statistics**

NDC: *See* **National Drug Codes**

NEC: *See* **not elsewhere classified**

Need for intervention: A term that relates to the severity-of-illness consequences that would result from the lack of immediate or continuing medical care

Need-to-know principle: The release-of-information principle based on the minimum necessary standard that means that only the information needed by a specific individual to perform a specific task should be released

Needs assessment: A procedure performed to determine what is required, lacking, or desired by an employee, a group, or an organization

Negative relationship: A relationship in which the effects move in opposite directions; *See* **inverse relationship**

Negligence: A legal term that refers to the result of an action by an individual who does not act the way a reasonably prudent person would act under the same circumstances

Neonatal death: The death of a liveborn infant within the first twenty-seven days, twenty-three hours, and fifty-nine minutes following the moment of birth

Neonatal mortality rate: The number of deaths of infants under twenty-eight days of age during a given time period divided by the total number of births for the same time period

Neonatal period: The period of an infant's life from the hour of birth through the first twenty-seven days, twenty-three hours, and fifty-nine minutes of life

Net: A term used in financial management to refer to the value of something, incorporating both the historical cost and anything that adds to or detracts from that value

Net assets: The organization's resources remaining after subtracting its liabilities

Net autopsy rate: The ratio of inpatient autopsies compared to inpatient deaths calculated by dividing the total number of inpatient autopsies performed by the hospital pathologist for a given time period by the total number of inpatient deaths minus unautopsied coroners' or medical examiners' cases for the same time period

Net death rate: The total number of inpatient deaths minus the number of deaths that occurred less than forty-eight hours after admission for a given time period divided by the total number of inpatient discharges minus the number of deaths that occurred less than forty-eight hours after admission for the same time period

Net income: The difference between total revenues and total expenses; *See* **profit**

Net loss: The condition when total expenses exceed total revenue

Net present value (NPV): A formula used to assess the current value of a project when the monies used were invested in the organization's investment vehicles rather than expended for the project; this value is then compared to the allocation of the monies and the cash inflows of the project, both of which are adjusted to current time

Net value: The purchase price of an item less its depreciation

Network: 1. A type of information technology that connects different computers and computer systems so that they can share information 2. Physicians, hospitals, and other providers who provide healthcare services to members of a managed care organization; providers may be associated through formal or informal contracts and agreements

Network administrators: The individuals involved in installing, configuring, managing, monitoring, and maintaining network computer applications and responsible for supporting the network infrastructure and controlling user access

Network computer: A type of thin client; a personal computer with a computer processing unit but no significant storage that is used to run programs on servers over a network rather than from programs stored on a hard disk

Network control: A method of protecting data from unauthorized change and corruption during transmission among information systems

Networking: The use of specific technology to connect disparate systems so they may share information

Network model: Type of health maintenance organization (HMO) in which the HMO contracts with two or more medical groups and reimburses the groups on a fee-for-service or capitation basis; *See* **group practice model**

Network protocol: A set of conventions that governs the exchange of data between hardware and/or software components in a communications network

Network provider: A physician or another healthcare professional who is a member of a managed care network

Neural networks: Nonlinear predictive models that, using a set of data that describe what a person wants to find, detect a pattern to match a particular profile through a training process that involves interactive learning

Neutral zone: Bridges's transitional stage in organizational change in which the past has been left but the future stage is not yet clearly established

New beginnings: Bridges's final stage of transition management in which the new organization is formed

Newborn (NB): An inpatient who was born in a hospital at the beginning of the current inpatient hospitalization

Newborn autopsy rate: The number of autopsies performed on newborns who died during a given time period divided by the total number of newborns who died during the same time period

Newborn bassinet count: The number of available hospital newborn bassinets, both occupied and vacant, on any given day

Newborn death rate: The number of newborns who died divided by the total number of newborns, both alive and dead

New patient: An individual who has not received professional services from the physician, or any other physician of the same specialty in the same practice group within the past three years

NGC: *See* **National Guideline Clearinghouse**

NIDSEC: *See* **Nursing Information and Data Set Evaluation Center**

NII-HIN: *See* **National Information Infrastructure-Health Information Network Program**

NLM: *See* **National Library of Medicine**

No carbon required (NCR): A designation indicating that a copy is unnecessary

Nomenclature: A recognized system of terms used in a science or art that follows preestablished naming conventions; a disease nomenclature is a listing of the proper name for each disease entity with its specific code number

Nominal group technique: A group process technique that involves the steps of silent listing, recording each participant's list, discussing, and rank ordering the priority or importance of items

Nominal level data: Data that fall into groups or categories that are mutually exclusive and with no specific order, for example patient demographics such as third party payer, race, and sex

Nonexempt employees: All groups of employees covered by the provisions of the Fair Labor Standards Act

Nonlicensed practitioner: A healthcare worker who does not hold a public license or certification and who is supervised by a licensed or certified healthcare professional in delivering care to patients

Nonmaleficence: A legal principle that means "do no harm"

Nonoperating room procedure: A type of procedure that is considered in assigning a diagnosis-related group but usually does not require the use of an operating room

Nonparametric technique: A type of statistical procedure used for variables that are not normally distributed in a population; *See* **distribution-free technique**

NonPARs: *See* **nonparticipating physicians**

Nonparticipant observation: A method of research in which researchers act as neutral observers who do not intentionally interact or affect the actions of the population being observed

Nonparticipating physicians (NonPARs): Physicians who treat Medicare beneficiaries but do not have a legal agreement with the program to accept assignment on all Medicare services and who, therefore, may bill beneficiaries more than the Medicare reasonable charge on a service-by-service basis

Nonparticipating provider: A healthcare provider who did not sign a participation agreement with Medicare and so is not obligated to accept assignment on Medicare claims

Nonprogrammed decision: A decision that involves careful and deliberate thought and discussion because of a unique, complex, or changing situation

Nonrandom sampling: A type of convenience or purposive sampling in which all members of the target population do not have an equal or independent chance of being selected for a research study

Nonroutine medical supplies: Supplies that are furnished either directly or under an arrangement with an outside supplier in which a home health agency, rather than the supplier, bills Medicare and the agency pays the supplier

No-RAP (request for anticipated payment) low-utilization payment adjustment: A type of claim submitted for an episode when home health agency is aware from the outset that the episode will require no more than four visits

Normal distribution: A theoretical family of continuous frequency distributions characterized by a symmetric bell-shaped curve, with an equal mean, median, and mode, any standard deviation, and with half of the observations above the mean and half below it

Normalization: 1. A formal process applied to relational database design to determine which variables should be grouped together in a table in order to reduce data redundancy across and within the table 2. Conversion of various representational forms to standard expressions so that those that have the same meaning will be recognized by computer software as synonymous in a data search

Normative decision model: A decision tree developed by Vroom-Yetton to determine when to make decisions independently or collaboratively or by delegation

North American Association of Central Cancer Registries (NAACCR): A national organization that certifies state, population-based cancer registries

NOS: *See* **not otherwise specified**

Nosocomial infection: An infection acquired by a patient while receiving care or services in a healthcare organization; *See* **hospital-acquired infection**

Nosocomial infection rate: The number of hospital-acquired infections for a given time period divided by the total number of inpatient discharges for the same time period

Nosology: The branch of medical science that deals with classification systems

Not elsewhere classified (NEC): A type of classification that indicates that there is no separate code for the condition even though the diagnostic statement is specific

Not otherwise specified (NOS): A type of classification that denotes a lack of information in the record and means unspecified rather than not elsewhere classified

Not-for-profit: A tax status under which excess revenues over expenses are used to enhance services to the community the organization serves rather to compensate the owners of the organization

Not-for-profit organization: An organization that is not owned by individuals, where profits may be held for a specific purpose or reinvested in the organization for the benefit of the community it serves

Notice of Privacy Practices: A statement (mandated by the HIPAA privacy rule) issued by a healthcare organization that informs individuals of the uses and disclosures of patient-identifiable health information that may be made by the organization, as well as the individual's rights and the organization's legal duties with respect to that information

Notice of Proposed Rulemaking (NPRM): Notice published in the *Federal Register* calling for public comment on its policy; the public at large has a specified time period to submit comments

Notifiable disease: A disease that must be reported to a government agency so that regular, frequent, and timely information on individual cases can be used to prevent and control future cases of the disease

NP: *See* **nurse practitioner**

NPDB: *See* **National Practitioner Data Bank**

NPF: *See* **national provider file**

NPI: *See* **national provider identifier**

NPRM: *See* **Notice of Proposed Rulemaking**

NPV: *See* **net present value**

NUBC: *See* **National Uniform Billing Committee**

NUCC: *See* **National Uniform Claim Committee**

Null hypothesis: A hypothesis that states there is no association between the independent and dependent variables in a research study

Numerical data: Data that include discrete data and continuous data

Numeric filing system: A system of health record identification and storage in which records are arranged consecutively in ascending numerical order according to the health record number

Nurse practitioner (NP): A healthcare professional authorized to provide basic primary healthcare, diagnosing and treating common acute illnesses and injuries

Nursing assessment: The assessment performed by a nurse to obtain clinical and personal information about a patient shortly after he or she has been admitted to a nursing unit

Nursing assessment record (NAR): A form used to track residents' functional status; supports the Minimum Data Set (MDS) process; *See* **activities of daily living (ADL) flow sheet**

Nursing facility: A comprehensive term for long-term care facilities that provide nursing care and related services on a twenty-four-hour basis for residents requiring medical, nursing, or rehabilitative care

Nursing Home Quality Initiative: A six-state pilot project performed in 2002 by the Centers for Medicare and Medicaid Services (CMS) that identifies quality measures that reflect the quality of care in nursing homes

Nursing Home Reform Act: A part of the Omnibus Budget Reconciliation Act of 1987 whose purpose is to guarantee the quality of nursing home care and to ensure that the care that residents receive helps them to achieve or maintain the "highest practicable" level of physical, mental, and psychosocial well-being

Nursing informatics: The field of information science concerned with the management of data and information used to support the practice and delivery of nursing care through the application of computers and computer technologies

Nursing Information and Data Set Evaluation Center (NIDSEC): The Nursing Information & Data Set Evaluation Center was established by the American Nurses Association (ANA) to review, evaluate against defined criteria, and recognize information systems from developers and manufacturers that support documentation of nursing care within automated Nursing Information Systems (NIS) or within computer-based patient record systems (CPR)

Nursing notes: Health record documentation that describes the nursing staff's observations of the patient and records the clinical and therapeutic services provided to the patient as well as the patient's response to treatment

Nursing vocabulary: A classification system used to capture documentation on nursing care

Nutritional assessment: The assessment performed by a registered dietitian to obtain information about a patient's diet history, weight and height, appetite and food preferences, and food sensitivities and allergies

NVAC: *See* **National Vaccine Advisory Committee**

NVSS: *See* **National Vital Statistics System**

OASIS: *See* **Outcomes and Assessment Information Set**

Object: The basic component in an object-oriented database that includes both data and their relationships within a single structure

Objective: A statement of the end result expected, stated in measurable terms, usually with a time limitation (deadline date) and often with a cost estimate or limitation

Objectivity: An accounting concept in which assets are classified at historical cost or current value

Object-oriented database (OODB): A type of database that uses commands that act as small, self-contained instructional units (objects) that may be combined in various ways

Object-oriented database management system (OODBMS): A specific set of software programs used to implement an object-oriented database

Object-oriented framework: A new way of programming and representing data that uses commands that act as small, self-contained instructional units that may be combined in various ways to produce larger programs

Object-relational database: A type of database (both object oriented and relational) that stores both objects and traditional tables

Object request broker (ORB): The messenger at the heart of the object-oriented framework that acts as a relay station between client and server

OBRA of 1987: *See* **Omnibus Budget Reconciliation Act of 1987**

OBRA of 1989: *See* **Omnibus Budget Reconciliation Act of 1989**

Observational research: A method of research in which researchers obtain data by watching research participants rather than by asking questions

Observational study: An epidemiological study in which the exposure and outcome for each individual in the study is observed

Observation patient: A patient who presents with a medical condition with a significant degree of instability and disability and who needs to be monitored, evaluated, and assessed to determine whether he or she should be admitted for inpatient care or discharged for care in another setting

Occasion of service: A specified identifiable service involved in the care of a patient that is not an encounter (for example, a lab test ordered during an encounter)

Occupancy percent/ratio: *See* **bed occupancy ratio**

Occupation: The employment, business, or course of action in which the patient is engaged

Occupational health: The degree to which an employee is able to function at an optimum level of well-being at work as reflected by productivity, work attendance, disability compensation claims, and employment longevity

Occupational health services: Health services involving the physical, mental, and social well-being of individuals in relation to their work and working environment

Occupational Safety and Health Act (OSHA) of 1970: The federal legislation that established comprehensive safety and health guidelines for employers

Occupational therapy (OT): A treatment that uses constructive activities to help restore the resident's ability to carry out needed activities of daily living and improves or maintains functional ability

Occurrence screening: A risk management technique in which the risk manager reviews the health records of current and discharged hospital inpatients with the goal of identifying potentially compensable events; *See* **generic screening**

OCE: *See* **outpatient code editor**

OCR technology: *See* **optical character recognition technology**

OD: *See* **organizational development**

Odds ratio: A relative measure of occurrence of an illness; the odds of exposure in a diseased group divided by the odds of exposure in a nondiseased group

OER: *See* **outcomes and effectiveness research**

Office of the Inspector General (OIG): The office through which the federal government established compliance plans for the healthcare industry

Offshoring: Outsourcing jobs to countries overseas, wherein local employees abroad perform jobs that domestic employees previously performed

Off-site storage policy: A policy that details how and when records are processed for shipment off-site

OIG: *See* **Office of the Inspector General**

OLAP: *See* **online analytical processing**

OLTP: *See* **online transaction processing**

Omnibus Budget Reconciliation Act (OBRA) of 1987: Federal legislation that required the Health Care Financing Administration (now renamed the Centers for Medicare and Medicaid Services) to develop an assessment instrument (called the resident assessment instrument) to standardize the collection of patient data from skilled nursing facilities

Omnibus Budget Reconciliation Act (OBRA) of 1989: The federal legislation that mandated important changes in the payment rules for Medicare physicians; specifically, the legislation that requires nursing facilities to conduct regular patient assessments for Medicare and Medicaid beneficiaries

One-tailed hypothesis: An alternative hypothesis in which the researcher makes a prediction in one direction

One-to-many relationship: A relationship that exists when one instance of an entity is associated with multiple instances of another entity

One-to-one relationship: A relationship that exists when an instance of an entity is associated with only one instance of another entity, and vice versa

Ongoing record review: A continuous health record quality review process performed by caregivers or HIM professionals to ensure that inpatient health records are complete and accurate and that the facility's clinical documentation practices meet relevant accreditation standards, state licensing laws, and federal regulatory requirements

Online analytical processing (OLAP): A data access architecture that allows the user to retrieve specific information from a large volume of data; *See* **online transaction processing**

Online transaction processing (OLTP): The real-time processing of day-to-day business transactions from a database; *See* **online analytical processing**

On-the-job training: A method of training in which an employee learns necessary skills and processes by performing the functions of his or her position

OODB: *See* **object-oriented database**

OODBMS: *See* **object-oriented database management system**

Open-ended HMO: *See* **point-of-service (POS) plan**

Open-ended question: *See* **unstructured question**

Open record: The health record of a patient who is still receiving services in the facility

Open-record review: A review of the health records of patients currently in the hospital or under active treatment; part of the Joint Commission on Accreditation of Healthcare Organizations (JCAHO) survey process

Open systems: Processes that are affected by what is going on around them and must adjust as the environment changes

Operating budget: The budget that summarizes the anticipated expenses for a department's routine, day-to-day operations

Operating clinician identification: The unique national identification number assigned to the clinician who performed the principal procedure

Operating room (OR): The area in a healthcare facility that is equipped and staffed to provide facilities and personnel for the performance of surgical procedures

Operating room (OR) procedure: A predefined procedure that usually requires the use of an operating room

Operating system: The principal piece of software in any computer system that consists of a master set of programs that manage the basic operations of the computer

Operation: *See* **surgical operation**

Operational budget: A type of budget that allocates and controls resources to meet an organization's goals and objectives for the fiscal year

Operational decision making: A process for addressing problems that come up in the day-to-day operation of a business unit or the day-to-day execution of a work task

Operational plan: The short-term objectives set by an organization to improve its methods of doing business and achieve its planned outcomes

Operation index: A list of the operations and surgical procedures performed in a healthcare facility that is sequenced according to the code numbers of the classification system in use

Operations analysis: *See* **workflow analysis**

Operations management: The application of mathematical and statistical techniques to production and distribution efficiency

Operations research (OR): A scientific discipline primarily begun during the Second World War that seeks to apply the scientific method and mathematical models to the solution of a variety of management decision problems

Operations support system (OSS): An information system that facilitates the operational management of a healthcare organization

Operative report: A formal document that describes the events surrounding a surgical procedure or operation and identifies the principal participants in the surgery

OPPS: *See* **outpatient prospective payment system**

Optical character recognition (OCR) technology: A method of encoding text from analog paper into bit-mapped images and translating the images into a form that is computer readable

Optical image–based system: A health record system in which information is created initially in paper form and then scanned into an electronic system for storage and retrieval

Optical imaging: The process by which information is scanned onto optical disks

OR: *See* **operating room**

OR: *See* **operations research**

OR procedure: *See* **operating room procedure**

Orange book: The common name for the U.S. Department of Defense document that defines the trusted computer system evaluation criteria, from which many of the security criteria for healthcare system are being drawn

ORB: *See* **object request broker**

Order entry: The use of a computer and decision support to record and initiate the transmission of a physician's order

Orders for restraint or seclusion: Physician's orders for physical or pharmaceutical restraint or seclusion to protect the patient or others from harm

Ordinal level data: Data with inherent order and with higher numbers usually associated with higher values

Organization: The planned coordination of the activities of more than one person for the achievement of a common purpose or goal

Organizational chart: A graphic representation of an organization's formal structure

Organizational development (OD): The application of behavioral science research and practices to planned organizational change

Organizational lifeline: A line drawing of important historical events in the life of an organization; used for organizational development intervention reflecting on historical trends

Organizational pull model: A model in which the organization views information systems technology as the means to enable people in the organization to work more efficiently and effectively

Orientation: A set of activities designed to familiarize new employees with their jobs, the organization, and its work culture

Orion Project: A Joint Commission on Accreditation of Healthcare Organizations initiative designed to assess accreditation models, develop a continuous accreditation process, and test alternative processes for reporting survey findings to hospitals

ORYX initiative: A Joint Commission on Accreditation of Healthcare Organizations initiative that supports the integration of outcomes data and other performance measurement data into the accreditation process

OSHA of 1970: *See* **Occupational Safety and Health Act of 1970**

OSS: *See* **operations support system**

Osteopath: A physician licensed to practice in osteopathy (a system of medical practice that is based on the manipulation of body parts as well as other therapies)

OT: *See* **occupational therapy**

OT: *See* **outlier threshold**

Other diagnoses: All conditions (recorded to the highest documented level of specificity) that coexist at the time of admission, develop subsequently, or affect the treatment received and/or length of stay

Other urban area: An urban area with a population of one million residents or fewer

Outcome: 1. The end result of healthcare treatment   2. The performance (or nonperformance) of one or more processes, services, or activities by healthcare providers

Outcome indicator: A measurement of the end results of a clinical process (for example, complications, adverse effects, patient satisfaction) for an individual patient or a group of patients within a specific diagnostic category; *See* **outcome measure**

Outcome measure: *See* **outcome indicator**

Outcomes analysis: *See* **outcomes assessment**

Outcomes and Assessment Information Set (OASIS): A standard core assessment data tool developed to measure the outcomes of adult patients receiving home health services under the Medicare and Medicaid programs

Outcomes and effectiveness research (OER): A type of research performed to explain the end results of specific healthcare practices and interventions

Outcomes assessment: An evaluation that measures the actual outcomes of patient care and service against predetermined criteria (expected outcomes), based on the premise that care is delivered in order to bring about certain results; *See* **outcomes analysis**

Outcomes management: The process of systematically tracking a patient's clinical treatment and responses to that treatment, including measures of morbidity and functional status, for the purpose of improving care; *See* **outcomes measurement**

Outcomes measurement: *See* **outcomes management**

Outcomes monitoring: *See* **outcomes management**

Outguide: A device used in paper-based health record systems to track the location of records removed from the file storage area

Outlier: 1. A case for which the costs are unusually high for the diagnosis-related group to which the case was assigned   2. An extreme statistical value that falls outside the normal range

Outlier payment: A payment made in addition to a full-episode payment when the cost of the services exceeds a fixed-loss threshold in the Medicare acute care prospective payment system

Outlier threshold (OT): The upper range (threshold) in length of stay before the case becomes a day outlier

Out-of-pocket expenses: Healthcare costs paid by the insured (for example, deductibles, copayments, and coinsurance) after which the insurer pays a percentage (often 80 or 100 percent) of covered expenses

Outpatient: A patient who receives ambulatory care services in a hospital-based clinic or department

Outpatient code editor (OCE): A software program linked to the Correct Coding Initiative that applies a set of logical rules to determine whether various combinations of codes are correct and appropriately represent the services provided

Outpatient coder: An individual responsible for assigning ICD-9-CM and CPT/HCPCS codes to ambulatory surgery or emergency department cases

Outpatient prospective payment system (OPPS): The Medicare prospective payment system used for hospital-based outpatient services and procedures that is predicated on the assignment of ambulatory payment classifications

Outpatient unit: A hospital-based ambulatory care facility organized into sections (clinics) whose number depends on the size and degree of departmentalization of the medical or clinic staff, available facilities, type of service needed in the community, and the needs of the patients for whom it accepts responsibility

Outpatient visit: A patient's visit to one or more units located in the ambulatory services area (clinic or physician's office) of an acute care hospital

Outsourcing: The hiring of an individual or a company external to an organization to perform a function either on site or off site

Outsourcing firm: A company that enters into a contract with a healthcare organization to perform services such as clinical coding

Overhead costs: The expenses associated with supporting but not providing patient care services

Owner's equity: The fund balance in a for-profit organization

P

A: *See* **physician assistant**

PACE: *See* **Programs of All-Inclusive Care for the Elderly**

Package Code: a code assigned by the manufacturer or private label distributor

Packaging: A payment under the Medicare outpatient prospective payment system that includes items such as anesthesia, supplies, certain drugs, and the use of recovery and observation rooms

Packet switching: An information transmission system in which data are encoded into short units (packets) and sent through an electronic communications network

PACS: *See* **picture archiving and communication system**

PAI: *See* **patient assessment instrument**

Palliative care: A type of medical care designed to relieve the patient's pain and suffering without attempting to cure the underlying disease

Panel interview: An interview format in which the applicant is interviewed by several interviewers at the same time

Paradigm: A philosophical or theoretical framework within which a discipline formulates its theories and makes generalizations

Parallel work division: A type of concurrent work design in which one employee does several tasks and takes the job from beginning to end

Parametric technique: A type of statistical procedure that is based on the assumption that a variable is normally distributed in a population

Parents and children: A name for exploding charges wherein the parent is the item that explodes into other items and appears on the bill

Pareto chart: A bar graph that includes bars arranged in order of descending size to show decisions on the prioritization of issues, problems, or solutions

PARs: *See* **participating physicians**

Partial episode payment (PEP) adjustment: A reduced episode payment that may be based on the number of service days in an episode

Partial hospitalization: A term that refers to limited patients stays in the hospital setting, typically as part of a transitional program to a less intense level of service; for example, psychiatric and drug and alcohol treatment facilities that offer services to help patients reenter the community, return to work, and assume family responsibilities

Participant observation: A research method in which researchers also participate in the observed actions

Participating physicians (PARs): Physicians who sign an agreement with Medicare to accept assignment for all services provided to Medicare beneficiaries for the duration of the agreement

Partnership: The business venture of two or more owners for whom the profits represent the owners' personal income

Part-time employee: An employee who works less than the full-time standard of forty hours per week, eighty hours per two-week period, or eight hours per day

PASARR: *See* **Preadmission Screening Assessment and Annual Resident Review**

Password: A series of characters that must be entered to authenticate user identity and gain access to a computer or specified portions of a database

Password crackers: Software programs used to identify an unknown or forgotten password

Path–goal theory: A situational leadership theory that emphasizes the role of the leader in removing barriers to goal achievement

Pathology report: A type of health record or documentation that describes the results of a microscopic and macroscopic evaluation of a specimen removed or expelled during a surgical procedure

Patient: A living or deceased individual who is receiving or has received healthcare services

Patient advocacy: The function performed by patient representatives (sometimes called ombudsmen) who respond personally to complaints from patients and/or their families

Patient assessment instrument (PAI): A standardized tool used to evaluate the patient's condition after admission to, and at discharge from, the healthcare facility

Patient care charting: A system in which caregivers enter data into health records

Patient care system: A type of information system that has traditionally been designed for nursing documentation

Patient-elected transfer: The elective transfer of a patient from one home health agency to another during a sixty-day episode

Patient health outcome: *See* **outcome**

Patient health record: *See* **health record**

Patient history questionnaire: A series of structured questions to be answered by patients to provide information to clinicians about their current health status; *See* **adult health questionnaire**

Patient-identifiable data: Personal information that can be linked to a specific patient, such as age, gender, date of birth, and address

Patient Self-Determination Act (PSDA): The federal legislation that requires healthcare facilities to provide written information on the patient's right to issue advance directives and to accept or refuse medical treatment

Patient's expected sources of payment: Regardless of payment method, the primary source expected to be responsible for the largest percentage of a patient's current bill

Patient's right to privacy: The justifiable expectation on the part of a patient that the information in his or her health record will be used only in the context of providing healthcare services

Patients' rights: The protections afforded to individuals who are undergoing medical procedures in hospitals or other healthcare facilities

Patient status code: A code that describes patient status at discharge or at the end of period in form locator 22 of the CMS-1450 form

Patient summary: *See* **problem list**

Payables: Outflows of cash

Payback period: A financial method used to evaluate the value of a capital expenditure by calculating the time frame that must pass before inflow of cash from a project equals or exceeds outflow of cash

Payer of last resort: A Medicaid term that means that Medicare pays for the services provided to individuals enrolled in both Medicare and Medicaid until Medicare benefits are exhausted and Medicaid benefits begin

Payment locality: A geographic pricing area historically used by Medicare carriers to calculate physicians' customary and prevailing charges for payment of Part B services

Payment status indicator (PSI): An alphabetic code assigned to CPT/HCPCS codes to indicate whether a service or procedure is to be reimbursed under the Medicare outpatient prospective payment system

PBX: *See* **private branch exchange**

PC: *See* **professional component**

PCG: *See* **physician care group**

PCM: *See* **primary care manager**

PCP: *See* **primary care physician**

PCP: *See* **primary care provider**

PCR: *See* **physician contingency reserve**

PDA: *See* **personal digital assistant**

PDCA cycle: *See* **Plan-Do-C-Act cycle**

PDSA cycle: *See* **plan-do-study-act cycle**

PE: *See* **physician extender**

Pediatric patient: A patient under the age of fourteen years

Pediatric service: A service that provides diagnostic and therapeutic services for patients under the age of fourteen years

Peer review: 1. An evaluation of professional performance by other people of equal standing within the same profession   2. The process by which experts in the field evaluate the quality of a manuscript for publication in a scientific or professional journal

Peer-reviewed journal: A type of professional or scientific journal for which content experts evaluate articles prior to publication; *See* **refereed journal**

Peer review organization (PRO): Until 2002, a medical organization that performs a professional review of medical necessity, quality, and appropriateness of healthcare services provided to Medicare beneficiaries; now called quality improvement organization (QIO)

Pending: A condition during which a facility waits for payment after a bill is dropped

PEP adjustment: *See* **partial episode payment adjustment**

Per case: A method of billing in which services are charged on the basis of the total service being rendered rather than by each component of the service (for example, charging for transplantation services when the organ has been procured, the transplant has been made, and aftercare has been rendered)

Percentage: A value computed on the basis of the whole divided into 100 parts

Percentage of occupancy: *See* **inpatient bed occupancy rate**

Per diem: Type of prospective payment method in which the third party payer reimburses the provider a fixed rate for each day a covered member is hospitalized

Per-diem rate: The cost per day derived by dividing total costs by the number of inpatient care days

Per-diem reimbursement: A reimbursement system based on a set payment for all of the services provided to a patient on one day rather than on the basis of actual charges

Per member per month: *See* **per patient per month**

Per patient per month (PPPM): A type of managed care arrangement by which providers are paid a fixed fee in exchange for supplying all of the healthcare services an enrollee needs for a specified period of time (usually one month but sometimes one year); *See* **per member per month (PMPM)**

Performance improvement (PI): The continuous study and adaptation of a healthcare organization's functions and processes to increase the likelihood of achieving desired outcomes

Performance indicator: A measure used by healthcare facilities to assess the quality, effectiveness, and efficiency of their services

Performance measure: A quantitative tool used to assess the clinical, financial, and utilization aspects of a healthcare provider's outcomes or processes

Performance measurement: The process of comparing the outcomes of an organization, work unit, or employee against preestablished performance plans and standards

Performance standards: The stated expectations for acceptable quality and productivity associated with a job function

Performance tests: *See* **ability tests**

Perinatal death: An all-inclusive term that refers to both stillborn infants and neonatal deaths

Periodic performance review (PPR): An organizational self-assessment conducted at the halfway point between triennial on-site accreditation surveys conducted by the Joint Commission on Accreditation of Healthcare Organizations

Peripheral: Any hardware device connected to a computer (for example, a keyboard, mouse, or printer)

Permanent employee: A person who is employed for an indefinite, ongoing period of time, typically long term

Permanent variance: A financial term the refers to the difference between the budgeted amount and the actual amount of a line item that is not expected to reverse itself during a subsequent period

Personal digital assistant (PDA): A hand-held microcomputer, without a hard drive, that is capable of running applications such as e-mail and providing access to data and information, such as notes, phone lists, schedules, and laboratory results, primarily through a pen device

Personal health record (PHR): An electronic or paper health record maintained and updated by an individual for himself or herself

Personal/unique identifier: The unique name or numeric identifier that sets apart information for an individual person for research and administrative purposes

PERT chart: *See* **program evaluation review technique chart**

Peter Principle: A cynical belief that employees will advance to their highest level of competence, and then be promoted to their level of incompetence where they will remain (named after the 1993 book by Laurence J. Peter)

PFA: *See* **priority focus area**

PFP: *See* **priority focus process**

PGP: *See* **pretty good privacy**

PHI: *See* **protected health information**

PHO: *See* **physician-hospital organization**

PHR: *See* **personal health record**

Physical: The actual organization of data in a system (for example, a single file divided into many pieces scattered across a disk); the opposite of logical

Physical access controls: 1. Security mechanisms designed to protect an organization's equipment, media, and facilities from physical damage or intrusion   2. Security mechanisms designed to prevent unauthorized physical access to health records and health record storage areas

Physical data model: The lowest level of data model with the lowest level of abstraction

Physical examination report: Documentation of a physician's assessment of a patient's body systems

Physical restraint: Any manual or mechanical device, material, or equipment attached or adjacent to a resident's body that restricts freedom of movement and prevents the resident's normal access to his or her own body

Physical therapy (PT): The field of study that focuses on physical functioning of the resident on a physician-prescribed basis

Physician assistant (PA): A healthcare professional licensed to practice medicine with physician supervision

Physician care group (PCG): Type of outpatient prospective payment method for physician services in which patients are classified into similar, homogenous categories

Physician champion: An individual who assists in educating medical staff on documentation procedures for accurate billing

Physician contingency reserve: *See* **withhold**

Physician extender (PE): A professional such as a physician assistant or nurse practitioner who "extends" the services of the physician to ensure continuity of care as issues or concerns arise in the long-term care setting and the physician cannot be present

Physician–hospital organization (PHO): An integrated delivery system formed by hospitals and physicians (usually through managed care contracts) that allows for cooperative activity but permits participants to retain some level of independence

Physician index: A list of patients and their physicians that is usually arranged according to the physician code numbers assigned by the healthcare facility

Physician–patient relationship: A relationship in which the physician trusts the patient to be forthcoming and honest in providing the information necessary for diagnosis and treatment and the patient trusts the physician to use that information responsibly and in his or her best interest and to protect it from becoming public knowledge

Physician payment reform (PPR): A legislative change in the way Medicare pays for physician services required by the Omnibus Budget Reconciliation Act of 1989, which includes a national fee schedule based on a resource-based relative value scale with geographic adjustments for differences in cost of practice, volume performance standards, and beneficiary protections

Physician practice management (PPM): A type of software that automates a physician office's patient appointment scheduling, registration, billing, and payroll functions

Physician profiling: A type of quality improvement and utilization management software that enables provider and payer organizations to monitor how and with what resources physicians are treating patients

Physician query process: A communication tool and educational mechanism that provides a clearer picture of specific resident diagnoses when in question

Physician query process policy: A policy that addresses request from physicians for additional information as part of the coding and reimbursement process

Physician's certification: A statement from a physician confirming a Medicare-eligible resident's need for long-term care services

Physician's order: A physician's written or verbal instructions to the other caregivers involved in a patient's care

Physiological signal processing systems: Systems that store vector graphic data based on the human body's signals and create output based on the lines plotted between the signals' points

Physiologic effects: cellular, tissue or organ processes or functions altered by drugs

PI: *See* **performance improvement**

Picture archiving and communication system (PACS): An integrated computer system that obtains, stores, retrieves, and displays digital images (in healthcare, radiological images)

Piece-rate incentive: An adjustment of the compensation paid to a worker based on exceeding a certain level of output

Pie chart: A graphic technique in which the proportions of a category are displayed as portions of a circle (like pieces of a pie)

Pilot study: A trial run on a smaller scale; *See* **feasibility study**

Pixel: An abbreviation for the term *picture element*, which is defined by many tiny bits of data or points

PKI: *See* **public key infrastructure**

Placebo: A medication with no active ingredients

Plain text: A message that is not encrypted

Plaintiff: The group or person who initiates a civil lawsuit

Plan-Do-C-Act (PDCA) cycle: A performance improvement model developed by Walter Shewhart, but popularized in Japan by W. Edwards Deming

Plan-do-study-act (PDSA) cycle: A performance improvement model designed specifically for healthcare organizations

Planned redundancy: A disaster recovery strategy in which information technology operations are duplicated at other locations

Planning: An examination of the future and preparation of action plans to attain goals; one of the four traditional management functions

Plan of care (POC): A term referring to Medicare home health services for homebound beneficiaries that must be delivered under a plan established by a physician

Platform: The combination of the hardware and operating system on which an application program can run

Plug-and-play: An adapter card hardware that sets connections through software rather than hardware, making hardware easier to install

PMPM: *See* **per member per month**

PMR: *See* **proportionate mortality ratio**

P/O: *See* **prosthetics and orthotics**

POC: *See* **plan of care**

Point and click: A means of data entry in which the user moves the computer's cursor by way of a mouse, up-and-down arrows, or some other pointing or navigational device to choose an icon or data element

Pointer: An item that has no dollar value and no code attached to it that is mapped to two or more items with separate charges

Point method: A method of job evaluation that places weight (points) on each of the compensable factors in a job whereby the total points associated with a job establish its relative worth and jobs that fall within a specific range of points fall into a pay grade with an associated wage

Point-of-care documentation: A system whereby information is entered into the health record at the time and location of service

Point-of-care information system: A computer system that captures data at the location (for example, bedside, exam room, or home) where the healthcare service is performed

Point-of-service (POS) plan: A type of managed care plan in which enrollees are encouraged to select healthcare providers from a network of providers under contract with the plan but are also allowed to select providers outside the network and pay a larger share of the cost; *See* **open-ended HMOs**

Policy: 1. A governing principle that describes how a department or an organization is supposed to handle a specific situation   2. Binding contract issued by a healthcare insurance company to an individual or group in which the company promises to pay for healthcare to treat illness or injury; *See* **health plan agreement** and **evidence of coverage**

Policyholder: An individual or entity that purchases healthcare insurance coverage; *See* **insured, certificate holder, member**, and **subscriber**

Polymorphic virus: A type of computer virus that can change its form after infecting a file

Population: The universe of data under investigation from which a sample is taken

Population-based registry: A type of registry that includes information from more than one facility in a specific geopolitical area, such as a state or region

Population-based statistics: Statistics based on a defined population rather than on a sample drawn from the same population

Position description: A document that outlines the work responsibilities associated with a job; *See* **job description**

Position power: A situation in contingency theory in which the leader is perceived as having the authority to give direction

Positive relationship: A relationship in which the effect moves in the same direction; *See* **direct relationship**

Positivism: *See* **quantitative approach**

POS plan: *See* **point-of-service plan**

Postdischarge plan of care: A care plan used to help a resident discharged from the long-term care facility to adapt to his or her new living arrangement

Postneonatal death: The death of a liveborn infant from twenty-eight days to the end of the first year of life (three hundred sixty-four days, twenty-three hours, fifty-nine minutes from the moment of birth)

Postneonatal mortality rate: The number of deaths of persons aged twenty-eight days up to, but not including, one year during a given time period divided by the number of live births for the same time period

Postoperative anesthesia record: Health record documentation that contains information on any unusual events or complications that occurred during surgery a well as information on the patient's condition at the conclusion of surgery and after recovery from anesthesia

Postoperative death rate: The ratio of deaths within ten days after surgery to the total number of operations performed during a specified period of time

Postoperative infection rate: The number of infections that occur in clean surgical cases for a given time period divided by the total number of operations within the same time period

Postterm neonate: Any neonate whose birth occurs from the beginning of the first day (two hundred ninety-fifth day) of the forty-third week following onset of the last menstrual period

Potentially compensable event: An event that may result in financial liability for a healthcare organization, for example, an injury, accident, or medical error

PPE: *See* **property, plant, and equipment**

PPO: *See* **preferred provider organization**

PPM: *See* **physician practice management**

PPPM: *See* **per patient per month**

PPR: *See* **periodic performance review**

PPR: *See* **physician payment reform**

PPS: *See* **prospective payment system**

Practice guidelines: Protocols of care that guide the clinical care process; *See* **Care Maps**, **critical paths**, and **clinical practice guidelines**

Practice without walls (PWW): *See* **group practice without walls**

Preadmission certification: *See* **prior approval (authorization)**

Preadmission review: *See* **prior approval (authorization)**

Preadmission Screening Assessment and Annual Resident Review (PASARR): A screening process for mental illness and mental retardation that must be completed prior to a prospective resident's admission to the long-term care facility

Preadmission utilization review: A type of review conducted before a patient's admission to an acute care facility to determine whether the planned service (intensity of service) or the patient's condition (severity of illness) warrants care in an inpatient setting

Preauthorization: *See* **prior approval (authorization)**

Preauthorization (precertification) number: Control number issued when a healthcare service is approved

Pre-certification: Process of obtaining approval from a healthcare insurance company before to receiving healthcare services; *See* **prior approval (authorization)**

Precision factor: The definitive tolerable error rate to be considered in calculations of productivity standards

Predecessor: A task that affects the scheduling of a successor task in a dependency relationship

Predictive modeling: A process used to identify patterns that can be used to predict the odds of a particular outcome based on the observed data

Preemption: In law, the principle that a statute at one level supercedes or is applied over the same or similar statute at a lower level, for example, the federal HIPAA privacy provisions trump the same or similar state law with certain exceptions

Pre-existing condition: Disease, illness, ailment, or other condition (whether physical or mental) for which, within a specified period before the insured's enrollment date of coverage, medical advice, diagnosis, care, or treatment was recommended or received; Healthcare coverage may be denied for a period of time for a pre-existing condition, but the Health Insurance Portability and Accountability Act constrains the use of exclusions for pre-existing conditions and establishes requirements exclusions for pre-existing conditions must satisfy

Preferred provider organization (PPO): A managed care arrangement based on a contractual agreement between healthcare providers (professional and/or institutional) and employers, insurance carriers, or third-party administrators to provide healthcare services to a defined population of enrollees at established fees that may or may not be a discount from usual and customary or reasonable charges

Preferred Term: In SNOMED CT, the most commonly used name or description assigned to a concept

Pregnancy Discrimination Act: The federal legislation that prohibits discrimination against women affected by pregnancy, childbirth, or related medical conditions by requiring that affected women be treated the same as all other employees for employment-related purposes, including benefits

Pregnancy termination: The birth of a liveborn or stillborn infant or the expulsion or extraction of a dead fetus or other products of conception from the mother

Premium: Amount of money that a policyholder or certificate holder must periodically pay an insurer in return for healthcare coverage

Preoperative anesthesia evaluation: An assessment performed by an anesthesiologist to collect information on a patient's medical history and current physical and emotional condition that will become the basis of the anesthesia plan for the surgery to be performed

Prescription management: Cost control measure that expands the use of a formulary to include patient education, electronic screening, alert, and decision-support tools, expert and referent systems, criteria for drug utilization, point-of-service order entry, electronic prescription transmission, and patient-specific medication profiles

Present value: A value that targets the current dollar investment and interest rate needs to achieve a particular investment goal

Preterm infant: An infant with a birth weight between 1000 and 2499 grams and/or a gestation between twenty-eight and thirty-seven completed weeks

Preterm neonate: Any neonate whose birth occurs through the end of the last day of the thirty-eighth week (two hundred sixty-sixth day) following onset of the last menstrual period

Pretty good privacy (PGP): A type of encryption software that uses public key cryptology and digital signatures

Prevalence rate: The proportion of people in a population who have a particular disease at a specific point in time or over a specified period of time

Prevalence study: *See* **cross-sectional study**

Preventive controls: Internal controls implemented prior to an activity and designed to stop an error from happening

Pricer: The software module in a Medicare claim-processing system that is used to determine charges under the prospective payment system

Primary analysis: The analysis of original research data by the researchers who collected them

Primary care: The continuous and comprehensive care provided at first contact with the healthcare provider in an ambulatory care setting

Primary care manager (PCM): The healthcare provider assigned to a TRICARE enrollee

Primary care physician (PCP): 1. Physician who provides, supervises, and coordinates the healthcare of a member and who manages referrals to other healthcare providers and utilization of healthcare services both inside and outside a managed care plan   2. The physician who makes the initial diagnosis of a patient's medical condition; *See* **primary care provider**

Primary care provider (PCP): Healthcare provider who provides, supervises, and coordinates the healthcare of a member; primary care physicians can be family and general practitioners, internists, pediatricians, and obstetricians/gynecologists; other PCPs are nurse practitioners and physician assistants; *See* **primary care physician**

Primary data source: A record developed by healthcare professionals in the process of providing patient care

Primary diagnosis: *See* **principal diagnosis**

Primary key: *See* **key field**

Primary patient record: *See* **health record**

Primary record of care: *See* **health record**

Primary source: An original work of a researcher who conducted an investigation

Principal diagnosis: The disease or condition that was present on admission, was the principal reason for admission, and received treatment or evaluation during the hospital stay or visit; *See* **most significant diagnosis**

Principal investigator: The individual with primary responsibility for the design and conduct of a research project

Principal procedure: The procedure performed for the definitive treatment of a condition (as opposed to a procedure performed for diagnostic or exploratory purposes) or for care of a complication

Prior approval (authorization): Process of obtaining approval from a healthcare insurance company before receiving healthcare services

Priority focus area (PFA): One of fourteen areas that the Joint Commission on Accreditation of Healthcare Organizations considers vital in the successful operation of a hospital; includes processes, systems, and structures that have a substantial effect on patient care services

Priority focus process (PFP): A process used by the JCAHO to collect, analyze, and create information about a specific organization being accredited in order to customize the accreditation process

Privacy: The quality or state of being hidden from, or undisturbed by, the observation or activities of other persons or freedom from unauthorized intrusion; in healthcare-related contexts, the right of a patient to control disclosure of personal information

Privacy Act of 1974: The legislation that gave individuals some control over information collected about them by the federal government

Privacy and security standards: Standards that ensure the confidentiality and integrity of patient-identifiable information

Privacy officer: The individual responsible for the development and implementation of an organization's privacy policies and procedures

Privacy rule: The federal regulations created to implement the privacy requirements of the simplification subtitle of the Health Insurance Portability and Accountability Act of 1996

Private branch exchange (PBX): A switching system for telephones on private extension lines that allows access to the public telephone network

Private key: In cryptography, an asymmetric algorithm restricted to one entity; *See* **cryptography; key; public key**

Private law: The collective rules and principles that define the rights and duties of people and private businesses

Private right of action: 1. The right of an injured person to secure redress for violation of his or her rights   2. A legal right to maintain an action growing out of a given transaction or state of facts and based thereon or a legal term pertaining to remedy and relief through judicial procedure

Private, unrestricted fee-for-service plan: A prepaid health insurance plan that allows beneficiaries to select private healthcare providers

Privilege: The professional relationship between patients and specific groups of caregivers that affects the patient's health record and its contents as evidence; the services or procedures, based on training and experience, that an individual physician is qualified to perform; a right granted to a user, program, or process that allows access to certain files or data in a system

Privileged communication: The protection afforded to the recipients of professional services that prohibits medical practitioners, lawyers, and other professionals from disclosing the confidential information that they learn in their capacity as professional service providers

Privileging process: The process of evaluating a physician's or other licensed independent practitioner's quality of medical practice and determining the services or procedures he or she is qualified to perform

PRO: *See* **peer review organization**

Probate court: A state court that handles wills and settles estates

Probationary period: A period of time in which the skills of a potential employee's work are assessed before he or she assumes full-time employment

Problem list: A list of illnesses, injuries, and other factors that affect the health of an individual patient, usually identifying the time of occurrence or identification and resolution; *See* **summary list** and **patient summary**

Problem-oriented health record: A way of organizing information in a health record in which clinical problems are defined and documented individually

Procedural codes: The numeric or alphanumeric characters used to classify and report the medical procedures and services performed for patients

Procedural risk: A professionally recognized risk that a given procedure may induce functional impairment, injury, morbidity, or mortality

Procedure: A document that describes the steps involved in performing a specific function

Procedures: The steps taken to implement a policy

Procedures and services (outpatient): All medical procedures and services of any type (including history, physical examination, laboratory, x-ray or radiograph, and others) that are performed pertinent to the patient's reasons for the encounter, all therapeutic services performed at the time of the encounter, and all preventive services and procedures performed at the time of the encounter

Process: A systematic series of actions taken to create a product or service; a formal writing (writ) issued by authority of law; any means used by the court to acquire or to exercise jurisdiction over a person or a specified property; a term from Donabedian's model of quality assessment that focuses on how care is provided

Process and workflow modeling: The process of creating a representation of the actions and information required to perform a function, including decomposition diagrams, dependency diagrams, and data flow diagrams

Process improvement team: An interdepartmental task force formed to redesign or change shared processes and procedures

Process indicators: Specific measures that enable the assessment of the steps taken in rendering a service

Product Code: The second segment of the National Drug Code, assigned by a firm

Productivity: A unit of performance defined by management in quantitative standards

Productivity bonus: A monetary incentive used to encourage employees to improve their output

Productivity software: A type of computer software used for word-processing, spreadsheet, and database management applications

Professional certification organizations: Private societies and membership organizations that establish professional qualification requirements and clinical practice standards for specific areas of medicine, nursing, and allied health professions

Professional component (PC): 1. The portion of a healthcare procedure performed by a physician 2. A term generally used in reference to the elements of radiological procedures performed by a physician

Professional standards review organization (PSRO): An organization responsible for determining whether the care and services provided to hospital inpatients were medically necessary and met professional standards in the context of eligibility for reimbursement under the Medicare and Medicaid programs

Profiling: A technique used to compare the activities of one or more healthcare providers

Profit: The difference between revenues and expenses used to build reserves for contingencies and long-term capital improvements; *See* **net income**

Profitability index: An index used to prioritize investment opportunities, where the present value of the cash inflows is divided by the present value of the cash outflows for each investment and the results are compared

Profit and loss statement: *See* **statement of revenue and expenses**

Pro forma: An estimate

Prognosis: The probable outcome of an illness, including the likelihood of improvement or deterioration in the severity of the illness, the likelihood for recurrence, and the patient's probable life expectancy

Program budget: *See* **milestone budget**

Program evaluation review technique (PERT) chart: A project management tool that diagrams a project's timelines and tasks as well as their interdependencies

Programmed decision: An automated decision made by people or computers based on a situation being so stable and recurrent that decision rules can be applied to it

Programmers: Individuals primarily responsible for writing program codes and developing applications, typically performing the function of systems development and working closely with system analysts

Programming language: A set of words and symbols that allows programmers to tell the computer what operations to follow

Programs of All-Inclusive Care for the Elderly (PACE): A state option legislated by the Balanced Budget Act of 1997 that provides an alternative to institutional care for individuals fifty-five years old or older who require the level of care provided by nursing facilities

Progress note: The documentation of a patient's care, treatment, and therapeutic response that is entered into the health record by each of the clinical professionals involved in a patient's care, including nurses, physicians, therapists, and social workers

Progressive discipline: A four-step process for shaping employee behavior to conform to the requirements of the employee's job position that begins with a verbal caution and progresses to written reprimand, suspension, and dismissal upon subsequent offenses

Prohibited abbreviations: Acronyms, abbreviations, and symbols that cannot be used in health records because they are prone to misinterpretation

Project charter: A document that defines the scope and goals of specific project; *See* **statement of work**

Project components: Related parameters of scope, resources, and scheduling with regard to a project

Project management: A formal set of principles and procedures that help control the activities associated with implementing a usually large undertaking to achieve a specific goal, such as an information system project

Project management software: A type of application software that provides the tools to track a project

Project network: The relationship between tasks in a project that determines the overall finish date

Project office: A support function for project management best practices

Project plan: A plan consisting of a list of the tasks to be performed in a project, a defined order in which they will occur, task start and finish dates, and the resource effort needed to complete each task

Project schedule: The portion of the project plan that deals specifically with task start and finish dates

Project team: A collection of individuals assigned to work on a project

Property, plant, and equipment (PPE): *See* **capital assets**

Proportion: A type of ratio in which the elements included in the numerator also must be included in the denominator

Proportionate mortality ratio (PMR): The total number of deaths due to a specific cause during a given time period divided by the total number of deaths due to all causes

Prosecutor: An attorney who prosecutes a defendant accused for a crime on behalf of a local, state, or federal government

Prospective payment: A method of determining reimbursement based on predetermined factors, not individual services

Prospective payment method: Type of episode-of-care reimbursement in which the third party payer establishes the payment rates for healthcare services in advance for a specific time period

Prospective payment system (PPS): A type of reimbursement system that is based on preset payment levels rather than actual charges billed after the service has been provided; specifically, one of several Medicare reimbursement systems based on predetermined payment rates or periods and linked to the anticipated intensity of services delivered as well as the beneficiary's condition; *See* **acute care prospective payment system, home health prospective payment system, outpatient prospective payment system,** and **skilled nursing facility payment system**

Prospective reimbursement: *See* **prospective payment system**

Prospective study: A study designed to observe outcomes or events that occur after the identification of a group of subjects to be studied

Prospective utilization review: A review of a patient's health records before admission to determine the necessity of admission to an acute care facility and to determine or satisfy benefit coverage requirements

Prosthetics and orthotics (P/O): A collective term that refers to the artificial extremities, augmentation devices, and mechanical appliances used in orthopedic care

Protected health information (PHI): Under HIPAA, all individually identifiable information, whether oral or recorded in any form or medium, that is created or received by a healthcare provider or any other entity subject to HIPAA requirements

Protective order: Any court order or decree whose purpose is to protect a person from personal harassment or service of process or discovery

Protocol: In healthcare, a detailed plan of care for a specific medical condition based on investigative studies; in medical research, a rule or procedure to be followed in a clinical trial; in a computer network, a protocol used to address and ensure delivery of data

Provider: Physician, clinic, hospital, nursing home, or other healthcare entity (second party) that delivers healthcare services

Provider-based entity: A provider of healthcare services, a rural health clinic, or a federally qualified health clinic, as defined in section 405-2401 of the *Code of Federal Regulations*, that is either created or acquired by a main provider for the purpose of furnishing healthcare services under the name, ownership, and administrative and financial control of the main provider, in accordance with the provisions of the proposed rule

Provider-based status: The relationship between a main provider and a provider-based entity or a department of a provider that complies with the provisions of the final rule on ambulatory payment classifications

Provider network organization: An organization that performs prospective, concurrent, and retrospective reviews of healthcare services provided to its enrollees

Provider-sponsored organization (PSO): Type of point-of-service plan in which the physicians that practice in a regional or community hospital organize the plan

PSDA: *See* **Patient Self-Determination Act**

PSI: *See* **payment status indicator**

PSO: *See* **provider-sponsored organization**

PSRO: *See* **professional standards review organization**

Psychiatric hospital: A hospital that provides diagnostic and treatment services to patients with mental or behavioral disorders

Psychiatry: The study, treatment, and prevention of mental disorders

Psychotherapy notes: Notes recorded in any medium by a mental health professional to document or analyze the contents of conversations between therapists and clients during private or group counseling sessions

PT: *See* **physical therapy**

Public assistance: A monetary subsidy provided to financially needy individuals; *See* **welfare**

Public health: An area of healthcare that deals with the health of populations in geopolitical areas, such as states and counties

Public health services: Services concerned primarily with the health of entire communities and population groups

Public key: In cryptography, an asymmetric algorithm made publicly available to unlock a coded message; *See* **cryptography; key; private key**

Public key infrastructure (PKI): A system of digital certificates and other registration authorities that verify and authenticate the validity of each party involved in a secure transaction

Public law: A type of legislation that involves the government and its relations with individuals and business organizations

Pull-down menu: The design of a data-entry screen of a computer in which categories of functions or structured data elements may be accessed through that category element

Pull list: A list of requests for records to be pulled for review during the audit process

Purchase order: A paper document or electronic screen on which all details of an intended purchase are reported, including authorizations

Purposive sampling: A strategy of qualitative research in which researchers use their expertise to select representative units and unrepresentative units to capture a wide array of perspectives

Push technology: A type of active computer technology that sends information directly to the end user as the information becomes available

PWW: *See* **practice without walls**

Q

DWIs: *See* **qualified disabled and working individuals**

QI: *See* **quality improvement**

QIO: *See* **quality improvement organization**

QIs: *See* **qualifying individuals**

QMBs: *See* **qualified Medicare beneficiaries**

Qualified disabled and working individuals (QDWIs): Medicare beneficiaries who are eligible for assistance, including disabled and working people who previously qualified for Medicare because of disability but lost entitlement because of their return to work despite the disability

Qualified Medicare beneficiaries (QMBs): Medicare beneficiaries who have resources at or below twice the standard allowed under the Social Security Income program and incomes at or below 100 percent of the federal poverty level

Qualifying individuals (QIs): Medicare beneficiaries whose incomes are at least 120 percent, but less than 175 percent, of the federal poverty level

Qualitative analysis: A review of the health record to ensure that standards are met and to determine the adequacy of entries documenting the quality of care

Qualitative approach: *See* **naturalism**

Qualitative standards: Service standards in the context of setting expectations for how well or how soon work or a service will be performed

Quality: The degree or grade of excellence of goods or services, including, in healthcare, meeting expectations for outcomes of care

Quality assurance: A set of activities designed to measure the quality of a service, product, or process with remedial action, as needed, to maintain a desired standard

Quality improvement (QI): A set of activities that measures the quality of a service or product through systems or process evaluation and then implements revised processes that result in better healthcare outcomes for patients, based on standards of care

Quality improvement organization (QIO): An organization that performs medical peer review of Medicare and Medicaid claims, including review of validity of hospital diagnosis and procedure coding information; completeness, adequacy, and quality of care; and appropriateness of prospective payments for outlier cases and nonemergent use of the emergency room; until 2002, called peer review organization

Quality indicator: A standard against which actual care may be measured to identify a level of performance for that standard

Quality review organization: A quality improvement organization or an accreditation organization

Quantitative analysis: A review of the health record to determine its completeness and accuracy

Quantitative approach: A philosophy of research that assumes that there is a single truth across time and place and that researchers are able to adopt a neutral, unbiased stance and establish causation; *See* **positivism**

Quantitative audit: An audit that compares a report of services billed for a specific client and within a specific time frame against the health record documentation; *See* **billing audit**

Quantitative standards: Measures of productivity in the context of setting expectations for how efficiently or effectively work will be performed

Quasi experimental design: *See* **causal-comparative research**

Questionnaire survey: A type of survey in which the members of the population are questioned through the use of electronic or paper forms

Queuing theory: An operations management technique for examining customer flow and designing ideal wait or scheduling times

Qui tam litigation: "Provisions within the law that allow for persons or entities with evidence of fraud against federal programs or contracts to sue the wrongdoer on behalf of the government" (Source: The False Claims Act Legal Center)

R

A: *See* **remittance advice**

Race: The major biological category to which an individual belongs as a result of a pedigree analysis or with which the individual identifies in cases where the data are inconclusive; usually includes American Indian/Eskimo/Aleut, Asian or Pacific Islander, black, white, other, and unknown/not stated

Radio frequency identification (RFID): An automatic recognition technology that uses a device attached to an object to transmit data to a receiver and does not require direct contact

Radioimmunoprecipitation assay (RIPA): One of the tests used to confirm a diagnosis of acquired immunodeficiency syndrome

RAI: *See* **resident assessment instrument**

RAID: *See* **redundant array of inexpensive disks**

Random sampling: An unbiased selection of subjects that includes methods such as simple random sampling, stratified random sampling, systematic sampling, and cluster sampling

Randomization: The assignment of subjects to experimental or control groups based on chance

Randomized clinical trial (RCT): A special type of clinical trial in which the researchers follow strict rules to randomly assign patients to groups

Range: A measure of variability between the smallest and largest observations in a frequency distribution

Ranked data: A type of ordinal data where the group of observations is first arranged from highest to lowest according to magnitude and then assigned numbers that correspond to each observation's place in the sequence

RAP: *See* **request for anticipated payment**

RAP: *See* **resident assessment protocol**

Raster image: A digital image or digital data made up of pixels in a horizontal and vertical grid or a matrix instead of lines plotted between a series of points

Rate: A measure used to compare an event over time; a comparison of the number of times an event did happen (numerator) with the number of times an event could have happened (denominator)

Rate of return method: A method used to justify a proposed capital expenditure in which the organization tries to find out what rate of return it would get if it invests in a particular project

Ratio: 1. A calculation found by dividing one quantity by another   2. A general term that can include a number of specific measures such as proportion, percentage, and rate

Ratio analysis: The mechanism by which a few basic ratios are applied to numbers obtained from financial statements, enabling comparisons to past and future performance trends and an opportunity to compare financial performance against industry benchmarks

Ratio level data: Data with a defined unit of measure, a real zero point, and with equal intervals between successive values; *See* **interval level data**

RAVEN: *See* **Resident Assessment Validation and Entry**

RBAC: *See* **role-based access control**

RBRVS: *See* **resource-based relative value scale**

R&C: *See* **reasonable and customary charges**

RCT: *See* **randomized clinical trial**

RDMS: *See* **relational database management system**

Read: An operation involving the flow of information from an object to a subject, without allowing alteration (which is the write function) of the information

Read codes: The former name of the United Kingdom's CTV3 codes; named for James Read, the physician who originally devised the system to organize computer-based patient data in his primary care practice; *See* **Clinical Terms, version 3 (CTV3)**

Readiness assessment: An evaluation of the status of a healthcare organization's infrastructure and culture in order to estimate the potential for successful implementation of a computer-based patient record

Read-only system: A system that is only able to copy data from a storage medium, such as a disk, to main memory and is not able to copy data from main memory to a storage medium

Real audio data: The storing, manipulating, and displaying of sound in a computer-readable format; *See* **sound data**

Reasonable and customary charges (R & C): The amounts charged by healthcare providers consistent with charges from similar providers for identical or similar services in a given locale; *See* **usual reasonable and customary charges**

Reasonable care: The degree of care that a reasonably prudent person would exercise in the same or similar circumstances

Rebasing: The redetermination of the ambulatory payment classification weights to reflect changes in relative resource consumption

Rebill: The act of resubmitting a corrected bill to the payer after it has been rejected

Recalibration: The adjustment of all ambulatory payment classification weights to reflect changes in relative resource consumption

Receivables: Amounts of money coming into the organization; **assets**

Records disaster recovery policy: A policy that establishes how records should be handled in a disaster such as a fire

Records purging policy: A policy that is used in conjunction with the off-site storage policy

Records removal policy: A policy that outlines how and when records may be removed from the health record department

Records retention policy: A policy that specifies the length of time that health records are kept as required by law

Recovery room record: A type of health record documentation used by nurses to document the patient's reaction to anesthesia and condition after surgery

Recruitment: The process of finding, soliciting, and attracting employees

Redisclosure: The process of releasing confidential health record information that was originally created and disclosed by another healthcare provider

Redundancy: The concept of building a backup computer system that is an exact version of the primary system and that can replace it in the event of a primary system failure

Redundant array of inexpensive disks (RAID): A method of ensuring data security

Reengineering: Fundamental rethinking and radical redesign of business processes to achieve significant performance improvements

Refereed journal: *See* **peer-reviewed journal**

Reference data: Information that interacts with the care of the individual or with the healthcare delivery system, such as a formulary, protocol, care plan, clinical alert, or reminder

Reference terminology: A set of concepts and relationships that provide a common consultation point for the comparison and aggregation of data about the entire healthcare process, recorded by multiple individuals, systems, or institutions

Referral: A request by a provider for a patient under the provider's care to be evaluated and/or treated by another provider

Referred outpatient: An outpatient who is provided special diagnostic or therapeutic services by a hospital on an ambulatory basis but whose medical care remains the responsibility of the referring physician

Refined case-based payment method: Case-based payment method enhanced to include patients from all age groups or from regions of the world with varying mixes of diseases and differing patterns of healthcare delivery

Reflective learning: A cycle of reflection, interpretation, application of learning, and action that is the basis of total quality management and other continuous improvement philosophies

Refreezing: Lewin's last stage of change in which people internalize new practices following transition

Regenstrief LOINC Mapping Assistant (RELMA): a free downloadable Microsoft Windows software download that provides LOINC users help in working with LOINC database files

Regional home health intermediaries (RHHI): Five fiscal intermediaries nationally designated to process Medicare home health and hospice claims

Registered health information administrator (RHIA): A type of certification granted after completion of an AHIMA-accredited four-year program in health information management and a credentialing examination

Registered health information technician (RHIT): A type of certification granted after completion of an AHIMA-accredited two-year program in health information management and a credentialing examination

Registered nurse (RN): A graduate nurse who has passed examinations for registration

Registry: A collection of care information related to a specific disease, condition, or procedure that makes health record information available for analysis and comparison

Regulation: A rule or order having the force of law issued by executive authority of the government

Rehabilitation: The process of restoring a disabled insured to maximum physical, mental, and vocational independence and productivity (commensurate with their limitations) through the identification and development of residual capabilities, job modifications, or retraining

Rehabilitation care: The process of restoring a disabled insured to maximum physical, mental, and vocation independence and productivity (commensurate with their limitations) through the identification and development of residual capabilities, job modifications, or retraining

Rehabilitation impairment categories (RICs): Groups of codes that indicate the primary cause of the rehabilitation hospitalization and are clinically homogeneous

Rehabilitation services: Health services provided to assist patients in achieving and maintaining their optimal level of function, self-care, and independence after some type of disability

Reimbursement: Compensation or repayment for healthcare services

Reinforcement: The process of increasing the probability of a desired response through reward

Rejection: The process of having a submitted bill not accepted by the payer, although corrections can be made and the claim resubmitted

Relational database: A type of database that stores data in predefined tables made up of rows and columns

Relational database management system (RDMS): A database management system in which data are organized and managed as a collection of tables

Relational online analytical processing (ROLAP): A data access methodology that provides users with various drill-down and business analysis capabilities similar to online analytical processing

Relationship: A type of connection between two terms

Relative risk (RR): A ratio that compares the risk of disease between two groups; *See* **risk ratio**

Relative value scale (RVS): Valuation or rating of physician services on the basis of relative physician resource inputs (work and other practice costs) to medical services; specifically refers to relative physician work values developed by the Harvard University relative value scale study

Relative value study (RVS): A guide that shows the relationship among the time, resources, competency experience, severity, and other factors necessary to perform procedures

Relative value unit (RVU): A measurement that represents the value of the work involved in providing a specific professional medical service in relation to the value of the work involved in providing other medical services

Relative weight (RW): 1. A multiplier that determines reimbursement 2. A measure of the resource intensity or clinical severity of a specific group of patients based on a specific case-mix methodology

Release and disclosure: The processes that make health record information available to legitimate users

Release of information (ROI): The process of disclosing patient-identifiable information from the health record to another party

Release of protected health information policy: A policy that outlines how residents and others may obtain copies of their health records

Reliability: A measure of consistency of data items based on their reproducibility and an estimation of their error of measurement

RELMA: *See* **Regenstrief LOINC Mapping Assistant**

Reminder: A prompt based on a set of rules that displays on the computer workstation, similar to a recommendation

Remittance advice (RA): An explanation of payments (for example, claim denials) made by third-party payers

Report cards: A method used by managed care organizations (and other healthcare sectors) to report cost and quality of care provided

Repository: A data structure where data are stored for subsequent use by multiple, disparate systems

Repudiation: A situation in which a user or system denies having performed some action, such as modifying information

Request for anticipated payment (RAP): The first of two Centers for Medicare and Medicaid Services forms used at the opening of a prospective payment system episode to ask for one of two split-percentage payments; not a claim according to Medicare statutes

Request for information (RFI): A written communication often sent to a comprehensive list of vendors during the design phase of the systems development life cycle to ask for general product information

Request for production: A discovery device used to compel another party to produce documents and other items or evidence important to a lawsuit

Request for proposal (RFP): A type of business correspondence asking for very specific product and contract information that is often sent to a narrow list of vendors that have been preselected after a review of requests for information during the design phase of the systems development life cycle

Requisition: A request from an authorized health record user to gain access to a medical record

Research data: Data used for the purpose of answering a proposed question or testing a hypothesis

Research method: The particular strategy used by a researcher to collect, analyze, and present data

Reserves: Unused profits from a not-for-profit organization that stay in the business

Residence: A patient's full address and zip code

Residency program: An accredited program whereby a hospital sponsors graduate medical education for physicians in training and, in the case of residencies in the clinical divisions of medicine, surgery, and other special fields, advanced training in preparation for the practice of a specialty

Resident: A common synonym for patient, especially in long-term care

Resident assessment instrument (RAI): A uniform assessment instrument developed by the Centers for Medicare and Medicaid Services to standardize the collection of skilled nursing facility patient data; includes the Minimum Data Set 2.0, triggers, and resident assessment protocols; *See* **Minimum Data Set**

Resident assessment protocol (RAP): A summary of a long-term care resident's medical condition and care requirements

Resident Assessment Validation and Entry (RAVEN): A type of data-entry software developed by the Centers for Medicare and Medicaid Services for long-term care facilities and used to collect Minimum Data Set assessments and to transmit data to state databases

Resident care facility: A residential facility that provides regular and emergency health services, when needed, and appropriate supporting services on a regular basis

Resident classification system: A system for classifying skilled nursing facility residents into mutually exclusive groups based on clinical, functional, and resource-based criteria

Residential arrangement: The situation in which an individual lives on a regular basis: owns a home or apartment; resides in a facility where health, disability, or aging related services or supervision are available; resides in another residential setting where no services are provided; resides in a nursing home or other health facility; resides in another institutional setting such as a prison; is homeless or lives in a shelter for the homeless; lives in a place unknown or not stated

Residential care: Services, including board and lodging, provided in a protective environment but with minimal supervision to residents who are not in an acute phase of illness and would be capable of self-preservation during an emergency

Residential care facility: A live-in facility that provides custodial care to persons unable to live independently because of a physical, mental, or emotional condition

Resident record: A term frequently used in long-term care in lieu of health record

Resident's right to access: A term encompassing the mechanisms in place to allow residents to review their own health information

Resolution: The degree of sharpness of a computer-generated image as measured by the number of dots per linear inch on a printout or the number of pixels across and down a display screen

Resource-based relative value scale (RBRVS): A Medicare reimbursement system implemented in 1992 to compensate physicians according to a fee schedule predicated on weights assigned on the basis of the resources required to provide the services

Resource intensity: The relative volume and types of diagnostic, therapeutic, and bed services used in the management of a particular illness

Resource Utilization Groups, Version III (RUG-III): A case-mix–adjusted classification system based on Minimum Data Set assessments and used by skilled nursing facilities

Resources: The labor, equipment, or materials needed to complete a project

Respiratory therapy (RT): The practice involved in enhancing respiratory function for the resident

Respite care: A type of short-term care provided during the day or overnight to individuals in the home or institution to temporarily relieve the family home caregiver

Responsibility: The accountability required as part of a job, such as supervising work performed by others or managing assets or funds

Responsibility center: A department as a whole, headed by an individual

Restitution: The act of returning something to its rightful owner, of making good or giving something equivalent for any loss, damage, or injury

Restorative nursing care: Care that incorporates resident-specific programs that restore and preserve function to assist the resident in maximizing functional independence and achieving a satisfactory quality of life

Resume: A document that describes a job candidate's educational background, work experience, and professional achievements

Retained earnings: Undistributed profits from a for-profit organization that stay in the business

Retention: 1. The process whereby inactive health records are stored and made available for future use in compliance with state and federal requirements   2. The ability to keep valuable employees from seeking employment elsewhere

Retention policy: A policy that establishes how long the healthcare facility should keep health records, the medium in which the information will be kept, and where the records will be located

Retention schedules: Timetables specifying how long various records are to be maintained according to rules, regulations, standards, and laws

Retrospective: A type of time frame that looks back in time

Retrospective coding: A type of coding that takes place after the patient has been discharged and the entire health record has been routed to the health information management department

Retrospective payment method: Type of fee-for-service reimbursement in which providers receive recompense after health services have been rendered

Retrospective review: The part of the utilization review process that concentrates on a review of clinical information following patient discharge

Retrospective study: A type of research conducted by reviewing records from the past (for example, birth and death certificates and/or health records) or by obtaining information about past events through surveys or interviews

Retrospective utilization review: A review of records some time after the patient's discharge to determine any of several issues, including the quality or appropriateness of the care provided

Return: The increase in value of an investment

Return on assets: The return on a company's investment, or earnings, after taxes divided by total assets

Return on equity (ROE): A more comprehensive measurement of profitability that takes into consideration the organization's net value

Return on investment (ROI): The financial analysis of the extent of value a major purchase will provide

Revenue: The charges generated from providing healthcare services; earned and measurable income

Revenue code: A three- or four-digit number in the chargemaster that totals all items and their charges for printing on the form used for Medicare billing

Revenue cycle: The process of how patient financial and health information moves into, through, and out of the healthcare facility, culminating with the facility receiving reimbursement for services provided

Revenue cycle management: A process whose ultimate goal is improved financial management, including an accelerated cash flow and lowered accounts receivable

Revocation: The act of withdrawing an authorization or permission that was previously granted

RFI: *See* **request for information**

RFID: *See* **radio frequency identification**

RFP: *See* **request for proposal**

RHHI: *See* **regional home health intermediaries**

RHIA: *See* **registered health information administrator**

RHIT: *See* **registered health information technician**

RICs: *See* **rehabilitation impairment categories**

Rider: Document added to a healthcare insurance policy that provides details about coverage or lack of coverage for special situations that are not usually included in standard policies; may function as an exclusion or limitation

RIPA: *See* **radioimmunoprecipitation assay**

Risk: 1. The possibility of injury or loss   2. The probable amount of loss foreseen by an insurer in issuing a contract

Risk adjustment: Any method of comparing the severity of illness of one group of patients with that of another group of patients; *See* **case-mix adjustment** and **severity-of-illness adjustment**

Risk analysis: An assessment of possible security threats to the organization's data; *See* **risk assessment**

Risk assessment: *See* **risk analysis**

Risk corridor: The limits established to prevent immediate large financial gains or losses for hospitals because of the implementation of a prospective payment system

Risk factor reduction: The reduction of risk in the pool of members

Risk management (RM): A comprehensive program of activities intended to minimize the potential for injuries to occur in a facility and to anticipate and respond to ensuing liabilities for those injuries that do occur

Risk of mortality (ROM): The likelihood of dying

Risk pool: The people in an insured group, their medical and mental histories, other factors such as age, and their predicted health

Risk prevention: One component of a successful risk management program

Risk sharing: An agreement in which a vendor assumes at least part of the responsibility, from a financial perspective, for the successful implementation of a computer system

Risk–transfer mechanism: A mechanism whereby risk is passed from a regulated insurer to a quasi-regulated, regulated, or nonregulated provider

RM: *See* **risk management**

RN: *See* **registered nurse**

ROE: *See* **return on equity**

ROI: *See* **release of information**

ROI: *See* **return on investment**

ROLAP: *See* **relational online analytical processing**

Role-based access control (RBAC): A control system in which access decisions are based on the roles of individual users as part of an organization

Role playing: A training method in which participants are required to respond to specific problems they may actually encounter in their jobs

Roles and responsibilities: The definition of who does what on a project and the hierarchy for decision making

ROM: *See* **risk of mortality**

Root-cause analysis: A technique used in performance improvement initiatives to discover the underlying causes of a problem

Routed generic: the combination of an active ingredient(s), or generic name, plus a route; useful in decision support functions for drug interactions to distinguish a topical drug, which may not interact with another drug, from its oral formulation, which may interact

Router: A device programmed to filter out or to allow certain types of data to pass through

Row: A set of columns or a collection of related data items in a table

RR: *See* **relative risk**

RT: *See* **respiratory therapy**

RUG-III: *See* **Resource Utilization Groups, Version III**

Rule induction: *See* **association rule analysis**

Rules and regulations: *See* **bylaws**

Rules engine: A computer program that applies sophisticated mathematical models to data that generate alerts and reminders to support healthcare decision making

Run chart: A type of graph that shows data points collected over time and identifies emerging trends or patterns

Rural area: Any area not designated as a metropolitan statistical area for the purposes of case-mix index sets and wage index adjustments to federal Medicare reimbursement rates

RVS: *See* **relative value scale**

RVS: *See* **relative value study**

RVU: *See* **relative value unit**

RW: *See* **relative weight**

RxNorm: A clinical drug nomenclature developed by the Food and Drug Administration, the Department of Veterans Affairs, and HL7 to provide standard names for clinical drugs and administered dose forms

Safety management: A system for providing a risk-free environment for patients, visitors, and employees

Sample: A set of units selected for study that represents a population

Sample size: The number of subjects needed in a study to represent a population

Sample size calculation: The qualitative and quantitative procedures to determine an appropriate sample size

Sample survey: A type of survey that collects data from representative members of a population

Sanctions: Penalties or other mechanisms of enforcement used to provide incentives for obedience with the law or with rules and regulations

Satellite clinic: A primary care facility, owned and operated by a hospital or other organization, which is located in an area convenient to patients or close to a specific patient population

Satisficing: A decision-making process in which the decision maker accepts a solution to a problem that is satisfactory rather than optimal

Scalable: The measure of a system to grow relative to various measures of size, speed, number of users, volume of data, and so on

Scalar chain: A theory in the chain of command in which everyone is included and authority and responsibility flow downward from the top of the organization

Scale: Measure with progressive categories, such as size, amount, importance, rank, or agreement

Scales of Measurement: A reference standard for data collection and classification; *See* **nominal level data, ordinal level data, interval level data, ratio level data** and **categorical data**

Scanning: The process by which a document is read into an optical imaging system

Scatter diagram: A graph that visually displays the linear relationships among factors

Scattergram: *See* **scatter plot**

Scatter plot: A visual representation of data points on an interval or ratio level used to depict relationships between two variables; *See* **scatter diagram** and **scattergram**

SCD: *See* **SNF clinical formulation**

SCDC: *See* **SNF drug component**

Scenarios: Stories describing the current and feasible future states of the business environment

Scheduling engine: A specific functionality in project management software that automates the assignment of task start-and-finish dates and, as a result, the expected project finish date

SCHIP: *See* **State Children's Health Insurance Program**

School special education: Specifically designed instruction provided by qualified teachers within the context of school with the goal of helping students acquire academic, vocational, language, social, and self-care skills (includes adapted physical education and the use of specialized techniques to overcome intrinsic learning deficits)

SCIC adjustment: *See* **significant change in condition**

Scientific inquiry: A process that comprises making predictions, collecting and analyzing evidence, testing alternative theories, and choosing the best theory

Scope: The amount of effort and materials needed to produce project deliverables

Scope creep: A process in which the scope of a project grows while the project is in process, virtually guaranteeing that it will be over budget and behind schedule

Scope of command: The number and type of employees who report to a specific management position in a defined organizational structure

Scope of work: The time period an organization is under contract to perform as a quality improvement organization

SCP: *See* **standard cost profile**

Screen prototype: A sketch of the user interface of each screen that is anticipated in a project

SDLC: *See* **systems development life cycle**

SDM: *See* **Semantic Data Model**

SDO: *See* **standards development organization**

Search engine: A software program used to search for data in databases (for example, a structured query language)

SEC: *See* **Securities and Exchange Commission**

Secondary analysis: A method of research involving analysis of the original work of another person or organization

Secondary care: A general term for healthcare services provided by a specialist at the request of the primary care physician

Secondary data source: Data derived from the primary patient record, such as an index or a database

Secondary diagnosis: A statement of those conditions coexisting during a hospital episode that affect the treatment received or the length of stay

Secondary patient record: A record, derived from the primary record, that contains selected data elements to aid nonclinical persons in patient care support, evaluation, or advancement

Secondary record: A record derived from the primary record and containing selected data elements

Secondary release of information: A type of information release in which the initial requester forwards confidential information to others without obtaining required patient authorization

Secondary source: A summary of an original work, such as an encyclopedia

Secondary storage: The permanent storage of data and programs on disks or tapes

Secondary variable: *See* **confounding variable**

Second opinion: Cost containment measure to prevent unnecessary tests, treatments, medical devices, or surgical procedures

Secure messaging system: A system that eliminates the security concerns that surround e-mail, but retains the benefits of proactive, traceable, and personalized messaging; *See* **secure notification delivery system**

Secure notification delivery system: *See* **secure messaging system**

Securities and Exchange Commission (SEC): The federal agency that regulates all public and some private transactions involving the ownership and debt of organizations

Security: 1. The means to control access and protect information from accidental or intentional disclosure to unauthorized persons and from unauthorized alteration, destruction, or loss   2. The physical protection of facilities and equipment from theft, damage, or unauthorized access; collectively, the policies, procedures, and safeguards designed to protect the confidentiality of information, maintain the integrity and availability of information systems, and control access to the content of these systems

Security audit process: A process put into place by a healthcare organization to monitor the effectiveness of its security program and to ensure compliance with it

Security breach: A violation of the policies or standards developed to ensure security

Security management: The oversight of facilities, equipment, and other resources, including human resources and technology, to reduce the possibility of harm to or theft of these assets of an organization

Security officer: The person assigned responsibility for managing the organization's information security program

Security program: A plan outlining the policies and procedures created to protect healthcare information

Security pyramid: A graphic representation of security measures in which each depends on the one below it

Security rule: The federal regulations created to implement the security requirements of the Health Insurance Portability and Accountability Act of 1996

Security standards: Statements that describe the processes and procedures meant to ensure that patient-identifiable health information remains confidential and protected from unauthorized disclosure, alteration, and destruction

Security threat: A situation that has the potential to damage a healthcare organization's information system

Self-directed learning: An instructional method that allows students to control their learning and progress at their own pace

Self-efficacy: The belief in one's capacity to organize and carry out a course of action to manage a situation

Self-insurance: Method of insurance in which the employer or other association itself administers the health insurance benefits for its employees or their dependents, thereby assuming the risks for the costs of healthcare for the group

Self-monitoring: The act of observing the reactions of others to one's behavior and making the necessary behavioral adjustments to improve the reactions of others in the future

Self-pay: A payer category in which the patient or patient's family, rather than a third-party payer (such as an insurance company), pays the bill for care

Self-reported health status: A method of measuring health status in which a person rates his or her own general health, for example, by using a five-category classification: excellent, very good, good, fair, or poor

Semantic Data Model (SDM): A natural application modeling mechanism that can capture and express the structure of an application environment; LOINC is an example of a semantic data model

Semantic differential scale: A measure that records a group's perception of a product, organization, or program through bipolar adjectives on a seven-point continuum, resulting in a profile

Semantic normal form (SNF): preferred terms for clinical drugs in RxNorm

Semantics: the meaning of a word or term; sometimes refers to comparable meaning, usually achieved through a standard vocabulary

Semistructured question: A type of question that begins with a structured question and follows with an unstructured question to clarify

Sensitivity label: A security level associated with the content of the information

Sentinel event: According to the JCAHO, an unexpected occurrence involving death or serious physical or psychological injury, or the risk thereof

Separate procedure: A procedure that is commonly part of another, more complex procedure, but which may be performed independently or be otherwise unrelated to the other procedure

Sequence diagram: A systems analysis tool for documenting the interaction between an actor and the information system

Serial filing system: A health record identification system in which a patient receives sequential unique numerical identifiers for each encounter with, or admission to, a healthcare facility

Serial numbering system: A type of health record identification and filing system in which patients are assigned a different but unique numerical identifier for every admission

Serial–unit numbering system: A health record identification system in which patient numbers are assigned in a serial manner but records are brought forward and filed under the last number assigned

Serial work division: A system of work organization where each task is performed by one person in sequence

Server: A type of computer that makes it possible to share information resources across a network of client computers

Service: An act performed by a person on behalf of another person

Service bonus: A monetary reward given to long-term staff in recognition of their skills and commitment to the organization

Service-line coder: A person who excels in coding one particular service line, such as oncology or cardiology

Services classification: Functionally autonomous units (departments, services, or divisions) of the medical staff organization in a hospital

Service utilization domain: The range of available services including the patient's use of inpatient services preceding home care admission and the receipt of rehabilitation therapies during the home health episode

Seven dimensions of data quality: The seven characteristics—relevancy, granularity, precision, timeliness, currency, consistency, and accuracy—used to evaluate the quality of data

Severity indexing: 1. The process of using clinical evidence to identify the level of resource consumption   2. A method for determining degrees of illness

Severity of illness (SI or SOI): A type of supportive documentation reflecting objective clinical indicators of a patient illness (essentially the patient is sick enough to be at an identified level of care) and referring to the extent of physiologic decompensation or organ system loss of function

Severity of illness adjustment: *See* **risk adjustment**

Severity-of-illness screening criteria: Standards used to determine the most appropriate setting of care based on the level of clinical signs and symptoms that a patient shows upon presentation to a healthcare facility

Severity-of-illness system: A database established from coded data on diseases and operations and used in the hospital for planning and research purposes

Severity weight (SW): A factor developed by 3M to indicate relative severity within every level in APR-DRGs and used to improve comparisons in profiling by severity-adjusted raw statistics

SGML: *See* **standard generalized markup language**

Shared systems: Systems developed by data-processing companies in the 1960s and 1970s to address the computing needs of healthcare organizations that could not afford, or chose not to purchase, their own mainframe computing systems

Shared Visions—New Pathways: The new accreditation process implemented by the Joint Commission on Accreditation of Healthcare Organizations in January 2004 and designed to focus on systems critical to the safety and quality of patient care, treatment, and services

Shareware: A type of software that is available from others, often on the Internet, for a nominal fee

Sheltered employment: An employment category provided in a special industry or workshop for the physically, mentally, emotionally, or developmentally handicapped

Shift differential: An increased wage paid to employees who work less desirable shifts, such as evenings, nights, or weekends

Short-stay patient: A patient admitted to the hospital for an intended stay of less than twenty-four hours and who is considered an outpatient and not included in inpatient hospital census statistics

SI: *See* **severity of illness**

Signal tracing data: *See* **vector graphic data**

Significance level: The criterion used for rejecting the null hypothesis

Significant change in condition (SCIC) adjustment: A single episode payment under multiple home health resource groups, each prorated to the number of service days delivered

Significant procedure: A procedure that is surgical in nature or carries a procedural or an anesthetic risk or requires specialized training

Significant procedure ambulatory payment classification: A procedure that constitutes the reason for the visit, dominates the time and resources rendered during the visit, and is not subject to payment reduction/discounting

Sign-on bonus: A monetary incentive used by a facility to encourage a candidate to accept employment

Signing out of health records internally to other facility departments: A collection of mechanisms to ensure that charts are tracked when taken out of the HIM department

Simon's decision-making model: A model proposing that the decision-making process moves through three phases: intelligence, design, and choice

Simple payback method: A method used to justify a proposed capital expenditure where the asset cost is divided by the net annual income of the asset to determine how long it will take for the asset to "pay back" what it cost the organization

Simple random sampling: The process of selecting units from a population so that each one has exactly the same chance of being included in the sample

Simulation: A training technique for experimenting with real-world situation by means of a computerized model that represents the actual situation

Simulation and inventory modeling: The key components of a plan that are computer simulated for testing and experimentation so that optimal operational procedures can be found

Simulation observation: A type of nonparticipant observation in which researchers stage events rather than allowing them to happen naturally

Simultaneous equations method: A budgeting concept that distributes overhead costs through multiple iterations, allowing maximum distribution of interdepartmental costs among overhead departments

Single-blinded study: A study design in which (typically) the investigator but not the subject, knows the identity of the treatment and control groups

Single sign-on: A type of technology that allows a user access to all disparate applications through one authentication procedure, thus reducing the number and variety of passwords a user must remember and enforcing and centralizing access control

Singleton ambulatory patient groups: An ambulatory patient group assigned to a patient claim that, after consolidation of significant procedures and packaging of ancillaries, is part of a visit with no remaining multiple significant procedures

Sixty-day episode payment: The basic unit of payment under home health prospective payment system that covers a beneficiary for sixty days regardless of the number of days furnished unless the beneficiary elects to transfer, has a significant change in condition, or is discharged and then returns to the same agency within the sixty-day episode

Skill: The ability, education, experience, and training required to perform a job task

Skilled nursing facility (SNF): A long-term care facility with an organized professional staff and permanent facilities (including inpatient beds) that provides continuous nursing and other health-related, psychosocial, and personal services to patients who are not in an acute phase of illness but who primarily require continued care on an inpatient basis

Skilled nursing facility (SNF) market basket index: An index consisting of the most commonly used cost categories for skilled nursing facility routine services, ancillary services, and capital-related expenses that reflects changes over time in the prices of an appropriate mix of goods and services included in covered skilled nursing facility services

Skilled nursing facility prospective payment system (SNF PPS): A per-diem reimbursement system implemented in July 1998 for costs (routine, ancillary, and capital) associated with covered skilled nursing facility services furnished to Medicare Part A beneficiaries

Sliding scale fee: A method of billing in which the cost of healthcare services is based on the patient's ability to pay

SLMBs: *See* **specified low-income Medicare beneficiaries**

SLP: *See* **speech-language therapy**

Small rural hospital: A hospital with fewer than one hundred beds that is located outside a medical savings account plan

Smart card: A credit card–sized piece of plastic on which is embedded a computer chip that may house data and processors for manipulating the data

SMI: *See* **supplemental medical insurance**

Sneakerware: A reference to the fact that secondary storage media must be physically moved from one location to another for data to be shared, which is a procedure still used by many healthcare organizations despite the extensive networking that exists today

SNF: *See* **semantic normal form**

SNF: *See* **skilled nursing facility**

SNF clinical formulation (SCD): One of the two types of semantic normal forms created in RxNorm for every clinical drug, the SCD consists of components and a dose form

SNF drug component (SCDC): One of the two types of semantic normal forms created in RxNorm for every clinical drug, the SCDC consists of an active ingredient and strength

SNF market basket index: *See* **skilled nursing facility market basket index**

SNF PPS: *See* **skilled nursing facility prospective payment system**

Sniffer: A software security product that runs in the background of a network, examining and logging packet traffic and serving as an early warning device against crackers; *See* **network analyzer** and **protocol analyzer**

SNODENT: *See* **Systematized Nomenclature of Dentistry**

SNOMED: *See* **Systemized Nomenclature of Human and Veterinary Medicine**

SNOMED CT: *See* **Systemized Nomenclature of Medicine Clinical Terminology**

SNOMED RT: *See* **Systemized Nomenclature of Medicine Reference Terminology**

Snowflake schema: A modification of the star schema in which the dimension tables are further divided to reduce data redundancy

SOAP: An acronym for a component of the problem-oriented medical record that refers to how each progress note contains documentation relative to subjective observations, objective observations, assessments, and plans

SOAPIER: A form of charting narrative notes that requires subjective, objective, assessment, plan, intervention, evaluation, and revision in the note structure

Socialization: The process of influencing the behavior and attitudes of a new employee to adapt positively to the work environment

Social Security Act of 1935: The federal legislation that originally established the Social Security program as well as unemployment compensation, and support for mothers and children; amended in 1965 to create the Medicare and Medicaid programs

Social Security number (SSN): A unique numerical identifier assigned to every U.S. citizen

Software: A program that directs the hardware components of a computer system to perform the tasks required

SOI: *See* **severity of illness**

Sole proprietorship: A venture with one owner in which all profits are considered the owner's personal income

Solo practice: A practice in which the physician is self-employed and legally the sole owner

Solvency: The state of being able to pay all debts

Sound data: *See* **real audio data**

Source of admission: The point from which a patient enters a healthcare organization, including physician referral, clinic referral, health maintenance organization referral, transfer from a hospital, transfer from a skilled nursing facility, transfer from another healthcare facility, emergency department referral, court or law enforcement referral, and delivery of newborns

Source of admission code: Form locator 20 on the CMS-1450 form

Source-oriented health record format: A system of health record organization in which information is arranged according to the patient care department that provided the care

Source systems: *See* **feeder systems**

Spaced training: The process of learning a task in sections separated by time

Span of control: The number of subordinates reporting to a supervisor

Special care unit: A medical care unit in which there is appropriate equipment and a concentration of physicians, nurses, and others who have special skills and experience to provide optimal medical care for critically ill patients or continuous care of patients in special diagnostic categories

Special cause variation: An unusual source of variation that occurs outside a process but affects it

S

Specialty software: A type of applications software that performs specialized, niche functions such as encoding or drawing and painting

Specific consent to treatment: A type of consent that explains the potential risks and benefits of a particular treatment or procedures and constitutes the resident's permission to the healthcare provider to perform the treatment or procedure

Specified low-income Medicare beneficiaries (SLMBs): Medicare beneficiaries who have resources similar to qualified Medicare beneficiaries, but higher incomes, although still less than 120 percent of the federal poverty level

Speech-language therapy (SLP): A treatment intended to improve or enhance the resident's ability to communicate and/or swallow

Speech recognition technology: Technology that translates speech to text

Spin-off: A new, separate company formed by a parent company whose shares are distributed to existing shareholders of the parent company in proportion to the new entity's relationship to the parent company

Split percentage payment: A type of reimbursement in which payments are made for each episode period and home health agencies receive two payments to make up the total permissible reimbursement for the episode

Sponsor: A person or an entity that initiates a clinical investigation of a drug (usually the drug manufacturer or research institution that developed the drug) by distributing it to investigators for clinical trials; a person in an organization that supports, protects, and promotes an idea within the organization; the company position with the ultimate responsibility for a project's success

SQL: See **structured query language**

SSN: See **Social Security number**

Stable monetary unit: The currency used as the measurement of financial transactions

Staff authority: The lines of reporting in the organizational chart in which the position advises or makes recommendations

Staff model health maintenance organization: A type of health maintenance that employs physicians to provide healthcare services to subscribers; See **closed panel**

Stage of neoplasm: A classification of malignancies (cancers) according to the anatomic extent of the tumor, such as primary neoplasm, regional lymph nodes, and metastases

Stages of grief: A five-stage model created by Kubler-Ross describing how people progress through loss to acceptance in response to death that may be applied to similar changes experienced by employees in response to organizational transition

Stakeholder: An individual within the company who has an interest in, or is affected by, the results of a project

Standard: 1. A scientifically based statement of expected behavior against which structures, processes, and outcomes can be measured   2. A model or example established by authority, custom, or general consent or a rule established by an authority as a measure of quantity, weight, extent, value, or quality

Standard cost profile (SCP): A set of data that identifies, analyzes, and defines the activities, including the costs, of departments within the organization to produce a service unit

Standard deviation: A measure of variability that describes the deviation from the mean of a frequency distribution in the original units of measurement; the square root of the variance

Standard generalized markup language (SGML): An International Standards Organization standard that establishes rules for identifying elements within a text document

Standard normal distribution: A normal distribution with a mean equal to zero and standard deviation equal to one; *See* **normal distribution**

Standard of care: An established set of clinical decisions and actions taken by clinicians and other representatives of healthcare organizations in accordance with state and federal laws, regulations, and guidelines; codes of ethics published by professional associations or societies; regulations for accreditation published by accreditation agencies; usual and common practice of equivalent clinicians or organizations in a geographical regions

Standard of law: A statute or regulation, or common practice, established by professional associations to identify what an individual is expected to do or not do in a given situation unless determined otherwise by a court

Standard risk: A person, who according to an insured's underwriting standards, is entitled to purchase insurance without paying an extra premium or incurring special restrictions

Standards development organization (SDO): A private or government agency involved in the development of healthcare informatics standards at a national or international level

Standards for privacy of individually identifiable health information: *See* **privacy rule**

Standard treatment protocols (STPs): Protocols that identify the specific service units necessary to produce a given product (patient)

Standing orders: Orders the medical staff or an individual physician has established as routine care for a specific diagnosis or procedure

Star schema: A visual method of expressing a multidimensional data structure in a relational database

State Children's Health Insurance Program (SCHIP): The children's healthcare program implemented as part of the Balanced Budget Act of 1997; sometimes referred to as the Children's Health Insurance Program, or CHIP

Statement: A list of unpaid invoices; sometimes a cumulative list of all transactions between purchaser and vendor during a specific time period

Statement of cash flow: A statement detailing the reasons why cash amounts changed from one balance sheet period to another; *See* **statement of changes in financial position**

Statement of changes in financial position: *See* **statement of cash flow**

Statement of changes in net assets: The accounting statement that explains the differences in net assets from period to period on the balance sheet

Statement of fund balance: *See* **statement of stockholder's equity**

Statement of operations: *See* **statement of revenue and expenses**

Statement of retained earnings: A statement expressing the change in retained earnings from the beginning of the balance sheet period to the end

Statement of revenue and expenses: A financial statement showing how much the organization makes or loses during a given reporting period; *See* **income statement, statement of operations, profit and loss statement,** and **earnings report**

Statement of stockholder's equity: A statement detailing the reasons for changes in each stockholder's equity accounts; *See* **statement of fund balance**

Statement of work: *See* **project charter**

State workers' compensation insurance funds: Funds that provide a stable source of insurance coverage for work-related illnesses and injuries and serve to protect employers from underwriting uncertainties by making it possible to have continuing availability of workers' compensation coverage

Statistical budget: A budget that provides measures of workload or activities in each department for the coming budget period

Statistical process control chart: A type of run chart that includes both upper and lower control limits and indicates whether a process is stable or unstable

Statistical significance: The probability that an observed difference is due to chance

Statute: A law enacted by a legislative body of a unit of government (for example, the U.S. Congress, state legislatures, and city councils)

Statute of limitations: A specific time frame allowed by a statute or law for bringing litigation

Statutory law: Written law established by federal and state legislatures; *See* **legislative law**

Stay outliers: *See* **outlier**

Stealth virus: A type of computer virus that can hide itself, making it difficult to locate

Stem and leaf plot: A visual display that organizes data to show its shape and distribution, using two columns with the stem in the left-hand column and all leaves associated with that stem in the right-hand column; the "leaf" is the ones digit of the number, and the other digits form the "stem"

Step-down allocation: A budgeting concept in which overhead costs are distributed once, beginning with the area that provides the least amount of non-revenue-producing services

Step-down unit: A unit used for cardiac patients for care between the cardiac intensive care unit and a general medical/surgical unit

Stillbirth: The birth of a fetus, regardless of gestational age, that shows no evidence of life (such as heartbeats or respirations) after complete expulsion or extraction from the mother during childbirth

Stop-loss benefit: Specific amount, in a certain timeframe such as one year, beyond which all covered healthcare services for that policyholder or dependent are paid at 100 percent by the healthcare insurance plan; *See* **maximum out-of-pocket cost** and **catastrophic expense limit**

Stop-loss insurance: A form of reinsurance that provides protection for medical expenses above a certain limit

Storyboard: A type of poster that includes text and graphics to describe and illustrate the activities of a performance improvement project

Storytelling: A group process technique in which group members create stories describing the plausible future state of the business environment

STPs: *See* **standard treatment protocols**

Straight numeric filing system: A health record filing system in which health records are arranged in ascending numerical order

Strategic communications: Programs created to advance specific organizational goals such as promoting a new center or service, establishing a new program, or positioning the organization as a center of excellence in a specific discipline such as cardiology or oncology

Strategic decision making: A type of decision making that is usually limited to individuals, such as boards of directors, chief executive officers, and top-level executives, who make decisions about the healthcare organization's strategic direction

Strategic goals: Long-term objectives set by an organization to improve its operations

Strategic information systems planning: A process for setting IS priorities within an organization; the process of identifying and prioritizing IS needs based on the organization's strategic goals with the intent of ensuring that all IS technology initiatives are integrated and aligned with the organization's overall strategic plan

Strategic issue: A question, topic, opportunity, or concern that is addressed through strategic management

Strategic management: The art and science of formulating, implementing, and evaluating cross-functional decisions that enable an organization to achieve its objectives

Strategic plan: A broad organizationwide plan by which the facility accomplishes its strategic goals

Strategic planning: A disciplined effort to produce fundamental decisions that shape and guide what an organization is, what it does, and why it does it

Strategy: A course of action designed to produce a desired (business) outcome

Strategy map: A visual representation of the cause-and-effect relationships among the components of an organization's strategy

Stratified random sampling: The process of selecting the same percentages of subjects for a study sample as they exist in the subgroups (strata) of the population

Streaming video: *See* **motion video**

Structure: A term from Donabedian's model of quality assessment that assesses an organization's ability to provide services in terms of both the physical building and equipment and the people providing the healthcare services

Structure and content standards: Common data elements and definitions of the data elements to be included in an electronic patient record

Structured analysis: A pattern identification analysis performed for a specific task

Structured data: Binary, computer-readable data

Structured data entry: A type of healthcare data documentation about an individual using a controlled vocabulary rather than narrative text

Structured decision: A decision made by following a formula or a step-by-step process

Structured interview: An interview format that uses a set of standardized questions that are asked of all applicants

Structured query language (SQL): A fourth-generation computer language that includes both DDL and DML components and is used to create and manipulate relational databases

Structured question: A type of question that limits possible responses; *See* **closed-ended question**

Structure indicator: A measurement that permits the assessment of an organization's capability to provide high-quality services

Subacute care: A type of step-down care provided after a patient is released from an acute care hospital (including nursing homes and other facilities that provide medical care, but not surgical or emergency care)

Subpoena: A command to appear at a certain time and place to give testimony on a certain matter

Subpoena duces tecum: A written document directing individuals or organizations to furnish relevant documents and records

Subpoena policy: A policy that outlines the steps required to handle the subpoena processing for protected health information

Subprojects: Smaller components of a larger project

Subrogation: The means by which an insurance company recovers moneys from a third party; that amount paid to or on behalf of an insurer, usually sought in respect to a loss (for example, an accident or injury)

Subscriber: Individual or entity that purchases healthcare insurance coverage; *See* **certificate holder, insured, member**, and **policyholder**

Successor: A task in a dependency relationship between two tasks that is dependent on the predecessor task

Summary list: *See* **problem list**

Summons: An instrument used to begin a civil action or special proceeding and is a means of acquiring jurisdiction over a party

Superbill: The office form used for physician office billing that is initiated by the physician and states the diagnoses and other information for each patient encounter

Supercomputer: The largest, fastest, and most expensive type of computer that exists today

Supervised learning: Any learning technique that has as its purpose to classify or predict attributes of objects or individuals

Supervisory managers: Managers who oversee small (two- to ten-person) functional workgroups or teams and often perform hands-on functions in addition to supervisory functions

Supplemental medical insurance (SMI) (Medicare Part B): A voluntary medical insurance program that helps pay for physicians' services, medical services, and supplies not covered by Medicare Part A

Supreme Court: The highest court in the U.S. legal system; hears cases from the U.S. Courts of Appeals and the highest state courts when federal statutes, treaties, or the U.S. Constitution is involved

Surgery: An umbrella term referring to the procedures of incision, excision, amputation, introduction, endoscopy, suture, and manipulation

Surgical operation: One or more surgical procedures performed at one time for one patient via a common approach or for a common purpose

Surgical package: A payment policy of bundling payment for the various services associated with a surgery into a single payment, covering professional services for preoperative care, the surgery itself, and postoperative care

Surgical procedure: Any single, separate, systematic process upon or within the body that can be complete in itself; is normally performed by a physician, dentist, or other licensed practitioner; can be performed either with or without instruments; and is performed to restore disunited or deficient parts, remove diseased or injured tissues, extract foreign matter, assist in obstetrical delivery, or aid in diagnosis

Surgical specialties: A group of clinical specialties that concentrates on the provision of surgical services by physicians who have received advanced training in obstetrics/gynecology, ophthalmology, orthopedics, cardiovascular surgery, otorhinolaryngology, trauma surgery, neurosurgery, thoracic surgery, urology, plastic and reconstructive surgery, anesthesiology, and pathology

Survey: A method of self-report research in which the individuals themselves are the source of the data

Survey feedback: An organizational development technique in which data on practices and attitudes are gathered and participants interpret them in order to plan change

SW: *See* **severity weight**

Swing beds: Hospital-based acute care beds that may be used flexibly to serve as long-term care beds

Synchronous: Occurring at the same time

Synergy: The interaction of parts to produce a greater outcome than would be obtained by the parts acting separately

Syntax: A term that refers to the comparable structure or format of data, usually as they are being transmitted from one system to another

System: A set of related and highly interdependent components that are operating for a particular purpose

Systematic literature review: Methodical approach to literature review the reduces the possibility of bias; characterized by explicit search criteria to identify literature, inclusion and exclusion criteria to select articles and information sources, and evaluation against consistent methodological standards; *See* **meta-analysis** and **integrative review**

Systematic sampling: The process of selecting a sample of subjects for a study by drawing every *n*th unit on a list

System catalog: An integrated data dictionary (which is a component of a database management system) that generally contains information on data tables and relationships in addition to data definitions

System design: The second phase of the systems development life cycle

System implementation: The third phase of the systems development life cycle

System infectors: Computer viruses that infect the system areas of diskettes or the hard drive of a computer; *See* **boot-record infectors**

Systematized Nomenclature of Dentistry (SNODENT): A comprehensive taxonomy that contains codes for identifying not only diseases and dental diagnoses but also anatomy, conditions, morphology and social factors that may affect health or treatment

Systematized Nomenclature of Human and Veterinary Medicine (SNOMED): A comprehensive clinical vocabulary developed by the College of American Pathologists that is the most promising set of clinical terms available for a controlled vocabulary for healthcare

Systemized Nomenclature of Medicine Clinical Terminology (SNOMED CT): A comprehensive, controlled clinical vocabulary developed by the College of American Pathologists

Systematized Nomenclature of Medicine Reference Terminology (SNOMED RT): A concept-based terminology consisting of more than 110,000 concepts with linkages to more than 180,000 terms with unique computer-readable codes

System maintenance and evaluation: The final phase of the systems development life cycle

System planning and analysis: The first phase of the systems development life cycle

Systems analysis and design: A performance improvement methodology that can be applied to any type of system

Systems analyst: An individual who investigates, analyzes, designs, develops, installs, evaluates, and maintains an organization's healthcare information systems; is typically involved in all aspects of the systems development life cycle; and serves as a liaison among end users and programmers, database administrators, and other technical personnel

Systems development life cycle (SDLC): A model used to represent the ongoing process of developing (or purchasing) information systems

Systems testing: A type of testing performed by an independent organization to identify problems in information systems

Systems theory: An approach to understanding organizations based on the organization and interconnections of its parts

Systems thinking: An objective way of looking at work-related ideas and processes with the goal of allowing people to uncover ineffective patterns of behavior and thinking and then finding ways to make lasting improvements

Table: An organized arrangement of data, usually in columns and rows

Table of allowances: *See* **fee schedule**

Tacit knowledge: The actions, experiences, ideals, values, and emotions of an individual that tend to be highly personal and difficult to communicate (for example, corporate culture, organizational politics, and professional experience)

Tactic: A method for accomplishing an end

Tactical decision making: A type of decision making that usually affects departments or business units (and sometimes policies and procedures) and includes short- and medium-range plans, schedules, and budgets

Tactical plan: A strategic plan at the level of divisions and departments

TANF: *See* **temporary assistance for needy families**

Target population: A large group of individuals who are the focus of a study

Task: The step to be performed in order to complete a project or part of a project

Task analysis: A procedure for determining the specific duties and skills required of a job

Task structure: A type of leadership orientation toward goals, production, and procedures

Tax Equity and Fiscal Responsibility Act of 1982 (TEFRA): The federal legislation that modified Medicare's retrospective reimbursement system for inpatient hospital stays by requiring implementation of diagnosis-related groups and the acute care prospective payment system

Taxonomy: The principles of a classification system, such as data classification, and the study of the general principles of scientific classification

TC: *See* **technical component**

TCP/IP: *See* **transmission control protocol/Internet protocol**

Team building: The process of organizing and acquainting a team, and building skills for dealing with later team processes

Technical component (TC): The portion of radiological and other procedures that is facility based or nonphysician based (for example, radiology films, equipment, overhead, endoscopic suites, and so on)

Technical skills: One of the three managerial skill categories, related to knowledge of the technical aspects of the business

Technology management: The planning and implementation of technological resources, as needed, to effectively and efficiently carry out the organization's mission

Technology push model: The view of information technology as being able to push organizations into new business areas

TEFRA: *See* **Tax Equity and Fiscal Responsibility Act of 1982**

Telecommunications: Voice and data communications

Telecommuting: A work arrangement (often used by coding and transcription personnel) in which at least a portion of the employee's work hours is spent outside the office (usually in the home) and the work is transmitted back to the employer via electronic means; *See* **telestaffing**

Telemedicine: A telecommunications system that links healthcare organizations and patients from diverse geographic locations and transmits text and images for (medical) consultation and treatment

Telephone callback procedures: Procedures used primarily when employees have access to an organization's health information systems from a remote location that verify whether the caller's number is authorized and prevent access when it is not

Telestaffing: *See* **telecommuting**

Template: A pattern used in computer-based patient records to capture data in a structured manner

Temporary assistance for needy families (TANF): A federal program that provides states with grants to be spent on time-limited cash assistance for low-income families, generally limiting a family's lifetime cash welfare benefits to a maximum of five years and permitting states to impose other requirements

Temporary budget variance: The difference between the budgeted and actual amounts of a line item that is expected to reverse itself in a subsequent period; the timing difference between the budget and the actual event

Temporary employee: A person who is employed for a temporary, definite period of time, such as to complete a specific project or to fill in for a permanent employee on vacation or other leave; or a person who is employed for an indefinite period of time but who receives none of the fringe benefits offered to permanent employees

Temporary National Codes: Codes established by insurers when a code is needed before the next January 1 annual update for permanent national codes; these codes are independent of the permanent national codes

Temporary privileges: Privileges granted for a limited time period to a licensed, independent practitioner on the basis of recommendations made by the appropriate clinical department or the president of the medical staff

Ten-step monitoring and evaluation process: The systematic and ongoing collection, organization, and evaluation of data related to indicator development promoted by the Joint Commission on Accreditation of Healthcare Organizations in the mid-1980s

Terminal: A term used to describe the hardware in a mainframe computer system by which data may be entered or retrieved

Terminal-digit filing system: A system of health record identification and filing in which the last digit or group of digits (terminal digits) in the health record number determines file placement

Terminology: A set of terms representing the system of concepts of a particular subject field; a clinical terminology provides the proper use of clinical words as names or symbols

Terminology standard: A terminology adopted by the appropriate standards-setting organizations for use in healthcare

Term neonate: Any neonate whose birth occurs from the beginning of the first day (two hundred sixty-seventh day) of the thirty-ninth week through the end of the last day of the forty-second week (two hundred ninety-fourth day), following onset of the last menstrual period

Term type (TTY): Each element of the normalized term in RxNorm

Tertiary care: A type of highly specialized care provided by specialists (such as neurosurgeons, fertility specialists, or immunologists) who use sophisticated technology and support services

Test statistics: A set of statistical techniques that examines the psychometric properties of measurement instruments

Text mining: The process of extracting and then quantifying and filtering free-text data

Text processing: The process of converting narrative text into structured data for computer processing

Textual: A term referring to the narrative nature of much of clinical documentation to date

Theory: A systematic organization of knowledge that predicts or explains the behavior or events

Theory X and Y: A management theory developed by McGregor that describes pessimistic and optimistic assumptions about people and their work potential

Therapy threshold: The total number of therapy visits (ten) for an episode of care in the Medicare system

Thin client: A computer with processing capability but no persistent storage (disk memory) that relies on data and applications on the host it accesses to be able to process data

Third opinion: Cost containment measure to prevent unnecessary tests, treatments, medical devices, or surgical procedures

Third–party administrator (TPA): A method by which an outside person or firm maintains all records, pays claims, and/or generally administers the benefits program of an employer group regarding the persons covered under the insurance plan

Third-party payer: An insurance company (for example, Blue Cross/Blue Shield) or healthcare program (for example, Medicare) that reimburses healthcare providers (second party) and/or patients (first party) for the delivery of medical services

Third party payment: Payments for healthcare services made by an insurance company or health agency on behalf of the insured

Threat: The potential for exploitation of a vulnerability

Three-dimensional imaging: The construction of pictures generated from computer data in three dimensions

360-degree evaluation: A method of performance evaluation in which the supervisors, peers, and other staff who interact with the employee contribute information

Time and motion studies: Studies in which complex tasks are broken down into their component motions to determine inefficiencies and to develop improvements

Time ladder: A form used by employees to document time spent on various tasks

Time period: A specific span of dates to which data apply

TOB: *See* **type of bill**

Token: A physical device, such as a key card, inserted into a door to admit an authorized person or into a computer to authenticate a computer user

Toll bypass: A circumvention of the public telephone toll system to avoid the usage fees charged by public carriers

T1: A digital phone line that can carry data at speeds of up to 1.544 megabits per second

Topography axis: Part of the body affected by disease

Topology: In networking terms, the physical or logical arrangement of a network

Tort: An action brought when one party believes that another party caused harm through wrongful conduct and seeks compensation for that harm

Tort laws: State legislation that applies to civil cases dealing with wrongful conduct or injuries

Total bed count days: The sum of inpatient bed count days for each of the days during a specified period of time

Total billed charges: All charges for procedures and services rendered to a patient during a hospitalization or encounter

Total inpatient service days: The sum of all inpatient service days for each of the days during a specified period of time

Total length of stay: The sum of the days of stay of any group of inpatients discharged during a specific period of time; *See* **discharge days**

Total quality management (TQM): A management philosophy that includes all activities in which the needs of the customer and the organization are satisfied in the most efficient manner by using employee potentials and continuous improvement

TPA: *See* **third-party administrator**

TQM: *See* **total quality management**

Tracer methodology: An evaluation that follows (traces) the hospital experiences of specific patients to assess the quality of patient care; part of the new Joint Commission on Accreditation of Healthcare Organizations survey process

Traditional fee-for-service (FFS) reimbursement: A reimbursement method involving third-party payers who compensate providers after the healthcare services have been delivered; payment is based on specific services provided to subscribers

Trainee: A person who is learning a task or skill

Trainer: A person who gives instruction on a task or skill

Training: A set of activities and materials that provide the opportunity to acquire job-related skills, knowledge, and abilities

Train-the-trainer: A method of training certain individuals who, in turn, will be responsible for training others on a task or skill

Trait approach: The belief that leaders possess a collection of traits or qualities that distinguish them from non-leaders

Transactional leadership: The leadership style of a manager who strives to maintain high levels of efficiency in an organization by balancing tasks with social orientation

Transaction-processing system: A computer-based information system that keeps track of an organization's business transactions through inputs (for example, transaction data such as admissions, discharges, and transfers in a hospital) and outputs (for example, census reports and bills)

Transactions: The individual events or activities that provide the basic input to the accounting process

Transaction standards: *See* **transmission standards**

Transcription: The process of deciphering and typing medical dictation

Transcriptionist: A specially trained typist who understands medical terminology and translates physicians' verbal dictation into written reports

Transfer: The movement of a patient from one treatment service or location to another; *See* **intrahospital transfer**

Transformational leadership: The leadership of a visionary who strives to change an organization

Transfusion record: Health record documentation that includes information on the type and amount of blood products a patient received and the patient's reaction to them

Transition: An ongoing plan used in establishing and maintaining the Medicare fee schedule

Transitional facility relative value unit: A blend of charge-based relative value units and resource-based relative expense for services provided in a facility setting

Transitional nonfacility relative value unit: A blend of charge-based relative value units and resource-based relative expense for services provided in a practice setting other than a facility, for example, a physician's office or freestanding clinic

Transmission control protocol/Internet protocol (TCP/IP): The multifaceted protocol suite, or open standard not owned by or proprietary to any company, on which the Internet runs

Transmission standards: Standards that support the uniform format and sequence of data during transmission from one healthcare entity to another; *See* **communication standards, messaging standards, and transaction standards**

Trauma center: An emergency care center that is specially staffed and equipped (usually with an air transport system) to handle trauma patients

Trauma hospitals: Hospitals with level-one trauma centers

Traumatic injury: A wound or injury included in a trauma registry

Treatment: The manipulation, intervention, or therapy; a broad term used by researchers to generically mean some act, such as a physical conditioning program, a computer training program, a particular laboratory medium, or the timing of prophylactic medications

Treatment difficulty: A term referring to the patient management problems that a particular illness presents to the healthcare provider, usually problems associated with illnesses without a clear pattern of symptoms, illnesses requiring sophisticated and technically difficult procedures, and illnesses requiring close monitoring and supervision

Treatment guidelines/protocols: *See* **clinical guidelines/ protocols**

Triage: 1. The sorting of, and allocation of treatment to, patients   2. An early assessment that determines the urgency and priority for care and the appropriate source of care

TRICARE: The federal healthcare program that provides coverage for the dependents of armed forces personnel and for retirees receiving care outside military treatment facilities in which the federal government pays a percentage of the cost; formerly known as Civilian Health and Medical Program of the Uniformed Services

TRICARE Extra: A cost-effective preferred provider network TRICARE option in which costs for healthcare are lower than for the standard TRICARE program because a physician or medical specialist is selected from a network of civilian healthcare professionals who participate in TRICARE Extra

TRICARE Prime: A TRICARE program that provides the most comprehensive healthcare benefits at the lowest cost of the three TRICARE options, in which military treatment facilities serve as the principal source of healthcare and a primary care manager is assigned to each enrollee

TRICARE Prime Remote: A program that provides active-duty service members in the United States with a specialized version of TRICARE Prime while they are assigned to duty stations in areas not served by the traditional military healthcare system

TRICARE Senior Prime: A managed care demonstration TRICARE program designed to better serve the medical needs of military retirees, dependents, and survivors who are sixty-five years old and over

TRICARE Standard: A TRICARE program that allows eligible beneficiaries to choose any physician or healthcare provider, which permits the most flexibility but may be the most expensive

Trier of fact: The judge or jury hearing a civil or criminal trial

Trigger: A documented response that alerts a skilled nursing facility resident assessment instrument assessor to the fact that further research is needed to clarify an assessment

Trim point: The length of stay threshold used in determining day outliers

Trojan horse: A destructive piece of programming code hidden in another piece of programming code (such as a macro or e-mail message) that looks harmless

TTY: *See* **term type**

Tunneling protocol: A protocol that ensures that data passing over a virtual private network are secure and operates as an outer envelope to an envelope with its enclosure

Turnkey product: A computer application that may be purchased from a vendor and installed without modification or further development by the user organization

Two-tailed hypothesis: A type of alternative hypothesis in which the researcher makes no prediction about the direction of the results

Type of bill (TOB): A form of coding that represents the nature of each form CMS-1450 claim

Type I error: A type of error in which the researcher erroneously rejects the null hypothesis when it is true

Type II error: A type of error in which the researcher erroneously fails to reject the null hypothesis when it is false

U

UACDS: *See* **Uniform Ambulatory Care Data Set**

UB-04: *See* **Uniform Bill-04**

UB-92: *See* **Uniform Bill-92**

UCR: *See* **usual, customary, and reasonable**

UDSMR: *See* **Uniform Data Set for Medical Rehabilitation**

UHDDS: *See* **Uniform Hospital Discharge Data Set**

UM: *See* **utilization management**

UM: *See* **utilization manager**

UMDNS: *See* **Universal Medical Device Nomenclature System**

UML: *See* **unified modeling language**

UMLS: *See* **Unified Medical Language System**

Unapproved abbreviations policy: A policy that defines the abbreviations that are unacceptable for use in the health record

Unbilled account: An account that has not been billed and is not included in accounts receivable

Unbundling: The practice of using multiple codes to bill for the various individual steps in a single procedure rather than using a single code that includes all of the steps of the comprehensive procedure

Uncontrollable costs: Costs over which department managers have little or no influence

Undercoding: A form of incomplete documentation that results when diagnoses or procedures are missing that should be coded

Understandable, reproducible, and useful (URU) principle: The guiding principal for modeling concepts in SNOMED CT, which states that all concepts must be understandable, reproducible, and useful

Unfavorable variance: The negative difference between the budgeted amount and the actual amount of a line item, where actual revenue is less than budget or where actual expenses exceed budget

Unfreezing: The first stage of Lewin's change process in which people are presented with disconcerting information to motivate them to change

Unified Medical Language System (UMLS): A program initiated by the National Library of Medicine to build an intelligent, automated system that can understand biomedical concepts, words, and expressions and their interrelationships

Unified modeling language (UML): A common data-modeling notation used in conjunction with object-oriented database design

Uniform Ambulatory Care Data Set (UACDS): A data set developed by the National Committee on Vital and Health Statistics consisting of a minimum set of patient/client-specific data elements to be collected in ambulatory care settings

Uniform Bill-04 (UB-04): The single standardized Medicare form for standardized uniform billing, scheduled for implementaton in 2007 for hospital inpatients and outpatients; this form will also be used by the major third-party payers and most hospitals

Uniform Bill-92 (UB-92): A Medicare form for standardized uniform billing; *See* CMS-1450

Uniform Code on Dental Procedures and Nomenclatures: *See* **Current Dental Terminology**

Uniform Data Set for Medical Rehabilitation (UDSmr): A data set operated within the Center for Functional Assessment Research, U.B. Foundation Activities, Inc., that collects data on patient age, sex, living situation prior to hospitalization, the impairment that is the primary reason for admission to a rehabilitation facility, and functional status at admission and discharge

Uniform Hospital Discharge Data Set (UHDDS): A core set of data elements adopted by the US Department of Health, Education, and Welfare in 1974 that are collected by hospitals on all discharges and all discharge abstract systems

Union: A collective bargaining unit that represents groups of employees and is authorized to negotiate with employers on the employees' behalf in matters related to compensation, health, and safety; *See* **labor organization**

Unique identifier: A type of information that refers to only one individual or organization

Unique personal identifier: A unique number assigned by a healthcare provider to a patient that distinguishes the patient and his or her medical record from all others in the institution, assists in the retrieval of the record, and facilitates the posting of payment

Unique physician identification number (UPIN): A unique numerical identifier created by the Health Care Financing Administration (now called the Centers for Medicare and Medicaid Services) for use by physicians who bill for services provided to Medicare patients

Unique provider identification number (UPIN): A unique number assigned by the Centers for Medicare and Medicaid Services to identify physicians and suppliers who provide medical services or supplies to Medicare beneficiaries

Unique user identifier: A unique identifier assigned to all authorized users of the health record and used to track users and log-in procedures

United Nations International Standards Organization (ISO): An international standards organization that coordinates all international standards development

Unit filing system: A health record filing system in which all inpatient and outpatient visits and procedures are arranged together under a permanent unit number

Unit numbering system: A health record identification system in which the patient receives a unique medical record number at the time of the first encounter that is used for all subsequent encounters

Unit work division: A method of work organization where each task is performed by one person at the same time that another person is doing a task, but one does not have to wait for the other

Unity of command: An human resources principle that assumes that each employee reports to only one specific management position

Univariate: A term referring to the involvement of one variable

Universal chart order: A system in which the health record is maintained in the same format while the patient is in the facility and after discharge

Universal Medical Device Nomenclature System (UMDNS): A standard international nomenclature and computer coding system for medical devices, developed by ECRI

Universal patient identifier: A personal identifier applied to a patient, such as a number or code, that is used permanently for many and varied purposes

Universal personal identifier: A unique numerical identifier for each citizen in the United States

Universal precautions: A set of procedures designed specifically to minimize or eliminate the spread of infectious disease agents from one individual to another during the provision of healthcare services

UNIX: An operating system developed by Bell Labs in the late 1960s, and one of the best systems for mission-critical applications

Unstructured analysis: A pattern identification analysis performed through a database without the specific goal of discovering interesting patterns that were not conceived previously

Unstructured data: Nonbinary, human-readable data

Unstructured decision: A decision that is made without following a prescribed method, formula, or pattern

Unstructured question: A type of question that allows free-form responses; *See* **open-ended question**

Unsupervised learning: Any learning technique that has as its purpose to group or cluster items, objects, or individuals

Upcoding: The practice of assigning diagnostic or procedural codes that represent higher payment rates than the codes that actually reflect the services provided to patients

Update: The annual adjustment to the Medicare fee schedule conversion factor

UPIN: *See* **unique physician identification number**

UPIN: *See* **unique provider identification number**

UR: *See* **utilization review**

Urban area: A metropolitan statistical area as defined by the Office of Management and Budget

Urgent admission: An admission in which the patient requires immediate attention for treatment of a physical or psychiatric problem

URU principle: *See* **Understandable, reproducible, and useful (URU) principle**

Use case: A technique that develops scenarios based on how users will use information to assist in developing information systems that support the information requirements

Use case diagram: A systems analysis technique used to document a software project from a user's perspective

User-based access: A security mechanism used to grant users of a system access based on identity

User groups: Groups composed of users of a particular computer system

U.S. Public Health Service: An agency of the U.S. Department of Health and Human Services that promotes the protection and advancement of physical and mental health

Usual, customary, and reasonable (UCR): Method of evaluating providers' fees in which the third party payer pays for fees that are "usual" in that provider's practice; "customary" in the community; and "reasonable" for the situation

Utility program: A software program that supports, enhances, or expands existing programs in a computer system, such as virus checking, data recovery, backup, and data compression

Utilization management (UM): 1. The planned, systematic review of the patients in a healthcare facility against care criteria for admission, continued stay, and discharge   2. A collection of systems and processes to ensure that facilities and resources, both human and nonhuman, are used maximally and are consistent with patient care needs

Utilization management organization: An organization that reviews the appropriateness of the care setting and resources used to treat a patient

Utilization manager (UM): Person that evaluates patient care, ensuring neither underutilization nor overutilization of resources

Utilization review (UR): The process of determining whether the medical care provided to a specific patient is necessary according to preestablished objective screening criteria at time frames specified in the organization's utilization management plan

Utilization Review Act: The federal legislation that requires hospitals to conduct continued-stay reviews for Medicare and Medicaid patients

Validity: 1. The extent to which data correspond to the actual state of affairs or that an instrument measures what it purports to measure   2. A term referring to a test's ability to accurately and consistently measure what it purports to measure

Valuation: The estimated market value of a project, an object, a merger, and so on

Values-based leadership: An approach that emphasizes values, ethics, and stewardship as central to effective leadership

Values statement: A short description that communicates an organization's social and cultural belief system

Variability: The dispersion of a set of measures around the population mean

Variable: A factor

Variable costs: Costs that change as output or volume changes in a constant, proportional manner

Variance: A measure of variability that gives the average of the squared deviations from the mean; in financial management, the difference between the budgeted amount and the actual amount of a line item; in project management, the difference between the original project plan and current estimates

V

Variance analysis: An assessment of a department's financial transactions to identify differences between the budget amount and the actual amount of a line item

V codes: A set of ICD-9-CM codes used to classify occasions when circumstances other than disease or injury are recorded as the reason for the patient's encounter with healthcare providers

Vector graphic data: Digital data that have been captured as points and are connected by lines (a series of point coordinates) or areas (shapes bounded by lines); *See* **signal tracing data**

Vendor system: A computer system developed by a commercial company not affiliated with the healthcare organization

Verification service: An outside service that provides a primary source check on information that a physician makes available on an application to the medical staff

Vertical dyad linkage: *See* **leader-member exchange**

Vertically integrated plan: *See* **integrated provider organization**

Vertically integrated system: *See* **integrated provider organization**

Vertical structure: The levels and relationships among positions in an organizational hierarchy

Videoconferencing: A communications service that allows a group of people to exchange information over a network by using a combination of video and computer technology

Virtual private network (VPN): A network established over a carrier's digital phone lines and dedicated solely to connecting several specific client sites

Virus: A computer program, typically hidden, that attaches itself to other programs and has the ability to replicate and cause various forms of harm to the data

Vision: A picture of the desired future that sets a direction and rationale for change

Vision statement: A short description of an organization's ideal future state

Visit: A single encounter with a healthcare professional that includes all of the services supplied during the encounter

Vital statistics: Data related to births, deaths, marriages, and fetal deaths

Vocabulary: A list or collection of clinical words or phrases and their meanings; *See* **controlled vocabulary**

Vocabulary mapping process: A process that connects one clinical vocabulary to another

Vocabulary standard: A common definition for medical terms to encourage consistent descriptions of an individual's condition in the health record

Vocational rehabilitation: The evaluation and training aimed at assisting a person to enter or reenter the labor force

Voiceover IP (VoIP): *See* **Internet protocol technology**

Voice recognition technology: *See* **continuous speech technology**

VoIP: *See* **Internet protocol technology**

Volume logs: Forms used (sometimes in conjunction with time ladders) to obtain information about the volume of work units received and processed in a day

Voluntary Disclosure Program: A program unveiled in 1998 by the OIG that encourages healthcare providers to voluntarily report fraudulent conduct affecting Medicare, Medicaid, and other federal healthcare programs

VPN: *See* **virtual private network**

Vulnerability: A weakness in a system that can be exploited to violate the system's intended behavior

Waiting period: Time between the effective date of a healthcare insurance policy and the date the healthcare insurance plan will assume liability for expenses related to certain health services, such as those related to preexisting conditions

WAN: *See* **wide-area network**

Web appliance: A computer without secondary storage capability that is designed to connect to a network

Web-based systems and applications: Systems and applications that use Internet technology

Web browser–based systems: Systems and applications written in one or more Web programming languages

Web content management systems: Systems in which information placed in a Web site can be labeled and tracked so that it can be easily located, modified, and reused

Web-enabled technology: A computer architecture that uses World Wide Web technology (for example, browsers that are client software programs designed to look at various kinds of Internet resources) developed for the Internet to connect systems and display data

Webmasters: Individuals who support Web applications and the healthcare organization's intranet and Internet operations

Web portal technology: offering a Web site entryway through which to access, find, and deliver information and including a broad array of resources and services, such as email, forums, and search engines

Web services: an open, standardized way of integrating disparate, Web browser-based and other applications

WEDI: *See* **Workgroup on Electronic Data Interchange**

Weight: The numerical assignment that is part of the formula by which a specific dollar amount, or reimbursement, is calculated for each diagnosis-related group or each ambulatory payment classification

Well newborn: A newborn born at term, under sterile conditions, with no diseases, conditions, disorders, syndromes, injuries, malformations, or defects diagnosed, and no operations other than routine circumcisions performed

Western blot: One of the tests used to confirm a diagnosis of acquired immunodeficiency syndrome

WHO: *See* **World Health Organization**

Wide-area network (WAN): A computer network that connects devices across a large geographical area

Windows: An operating system product made by Microsoft that is easy to learn and user-friendly because all applications that run on it have a similar, pictorial appearance, and movement among various applications is made available through multiple, simultaneous views

Wireless local-area network (WLAN): A data transmission network that uses an unguided medium such as radio waves or microwaves

Wireless technology: A type of technology that uses wireless networks and wireless devices to access and transmit data in real time

Wisdom: The intelligence that gives individuals the empowerment and courage to act

Withhold: Portion of providers' capitated payments that managed care organizations deduct and hold in order to create an incentive for efficient or reduced utilization of healthcare services; *See* **physician contingency reserve**

Withhold pool: Aggregate amount withheld from all providers' capitation payments as an amount to cover expenditures in excess of targets

W

WLAN: *See* **wireless local-area network**

Word-processing services: Companies outside the health-care facility that specialize in the deciphering and typing of medical dictation

Work: The effort, usually described in hours, needed to complete a task

Workaround: A series of unnatural steps taken to compensate for either poorly performing software or the lack of desire to use a computer

Work breakdown structure: A hierarchical structure that decomposes project activities into levels of detail

Work distribution analysis: An analysis used to determine whether a department's current work assignments and job content are appropriate

Work distribution chart: A matrix that depicts the work being done in a particular workgroup in terms of specific tasks and activities, time spent on tasks, and the employees performing the tasks

Work division: The way in which tasks are handled within an organization

Worker Immaturity–Maturity: The model developed by Argyris to describe how leadership should change with an employee's maturity

Workers' compensation: The medical and income insurance coverage for certain employees in unusually hazardous jobs

Workflow: Any work process that must be handled by more than one person

Workflow analysis: A technique used to study the flow of operations for automation; *See* **operations analysis**

Workflow technology: Technology that allows computers to add and extract value from document content as the documents move throughout an organization

Workgroup on Electronic Data Interchange (WEDI): A subgroup of Accreditation Standards Committee X12 that has been involved in developing electronic data interchange standards for billing transactions

Working conditions: The environment in which work is performed (surroundings) and the physical dangers or risks involved in performing the job (hazards)

Work imaging study: A technique used to analyze the coding time required of full-time equivalent employees (FTEs) compared with established productivity standards

Work measurement: The process of studying the amount of work accomplished and how long it takes to accomplish work in order to define and monitor productivity

Work products: Documents produced during the completion of a task that may be a component of, or contribute to, a project deliverable

Work sampling: A work measurement technique that uses random sample measurements to characterize the performance of the whole

Workstation: A computer designed to accept data from multiple sources in order to assist in managing information for daily activities and to provide a convenient means of entering data as desired by the user at the point of care; *See* **intelligent workstation**

World Health Organization (WHO): The United Nations specialized agency for health, established on April 7, 1948, with the objective, as set out in its constitution, of the attainment by all peoples of the highest possible levels of health; responsible for *The International Statistical Classification of Diseases & Related Health Problems* **(ICD-10)**

World Wide Web: A portion of the Internet that connects large databases and servers to support electronic mail and other communications

Worm: A special type of computer virus, usually transferred from computer to computer via e-mail, that can replicate itself and use memory but cannot attach itself to other programs

Write-off: The action taken to eliminate the balance of a bill after the bill has been submitted and partial payment has been made or payment has been denied and all avenues of collecting the payment have been exhausted

W-10: *See* **interagency transfer form**

*X***-axis:** The horizontal axis on a graph where the independent variables are noted

XML: *See* **extensible markup language**

*Y***-axis:** The vertical axis on a graph that displays frequency

Years of schooling: The highest grade of schooling completed by the enrollee or patient

Y2K compliance: The testing and correcting of information systems and devices that rely on a two-digit date field for the calculation of dates, which produces errors when calculating dates from the year 2000 forward

Zero balance: The result of writing off the balance of an account, which closes off the account and ends the days in accounts receivable

Zero-based budgets: Types of budgets in which each budget cycle poses the opportunity to continue or discontinue services based on available resources so that every department or activity must be justified and prioritized annually to effectively allocate resources